EDWARD S. CURTIS
The Sioux and the Apsaroke

From Volumes Three and Four of *The North American Indian*

Edited by Stuart Zoll   Foreword by A. D. Coleman

Harper COLOPHON BOOKS/CN 380/$4.95

The Sioux and the Apsaroke

THE MEDICINE-MAN

EDWARD S. CURTIS

The Sioux and the Apsaroke

From Volumes Three and Four of
The North American Indian

Edited by Stuart Zoll
Foreword by A. D. Coleman

Harper Colophon Books
HARPER & ROW, PUBLISHERS
NEW YORK, EVANSTON, SAN FRANCISCO, LONDON

THE SIOUX AND THE APSAROKE: FROM VOLUMES III AND IV OF *THE NORTH AMERICAN INDIAN* BY EDWARD S. CURTIS

Copyright © 1975 by Stuart Zoll. FOREWORD Copyright © 1975 by A. D. Coleman. All rights reserved. Printed in the United States of America. No part of this book may be used or reproduced in any manner without written permission except in the case of brief quotations embodied in critical aricles and reviews. For information address Harper & Row, Publishers, Inc., 10 East 53d Street, New York, N.Y. 10022. Published simultaneously in Canada by Fitzhenry & Whiteside Limited, Toronto.

First HARPER COLOPHON edition published 1975

LIBRARY OF CONGRESS CATALOG CARD NUMBER: 75-781

STANDARD BOOK NUMBER: 06-090380-5

75 76 77 78 79 10 9 8 7 6 5 4 3 2 1

ACKNOWLEDGMENT

This book is dedicated to the Sioux and Apsaroke
Indians, and to all the aboriginal tribes of the world
that have vanished under the heels of "progress."

And to my dearest friends, John Graff and Bob Lee,
who first introduced me to the powerful magic of Edward S. Curtis.

Special thanks to the collectors who loaned me gravures from their private
collections and waited patiently for the completion of this book:
Mark Zapplin - Curtis Gravures, Boulder, Colo.
Paul Lodi - Conjectures, Gould, Lodi, & Boyton, Brighton, Mass.
John Sodegren - Cambridge, Mass.
Curtis Ltd. - Box 379, Phoenicia, N.Y.

CONTENTS

CONTENTS

ILLUSTRATIONS

ILLUSTRATIONS

FOREWORD

It seems the more we learn about Edward Sherriff Curtis, the more we find there is to know.

As recently as five years ago, we knew far less than we do now. At that time, the name of Edward S. Curtis was so unfamiliar that it appeared in none of the standard histories of photography. His magnum opus, *The North American Indian,* had slipped into an almost total obscurity (for which its own scope, size, and lavishness of production were partly to blame). His writings were out of print, and his images were never exhibited. In all, it was virtually as if Curtis had never existed, as if his work had never been accomplished.

Today the situation is considerably different. Half a dozen books anthologizing Curtis's images have been published, with more doubtless on the way. A documentary film on his life and work has been completed. His original photographs, and the superb gravure prints which were made therefrom, have been presented anew in dozens of museum and gallery exhibitions, not only across the United States and Canada but in Europe as well. As a complete set, *The North American Indian* now fetches unprecedented five-figure prices, while individual prints of his images have become collector's items. There is even a recently founded mail-order club selling new prints "hand-pulled from the authenticated antique Curtis copperplates." Without a doubt, we are in the midst of a Curtis renaissance.

The first phase of this renaissance, which began with an exhibit of gravures from *The North American Indian* at the Pierpont Morgan Library in New York during the fall of 1971, was a rediscovery of Curtis the photographer.

Since his obituary in the New York Times in 1952 mentioned Curtis's photographic work only once, and then in passing, it is ironic that it should have been that facet of his endeavor which restored him to the fame he so deserves. However, his photographs — well over two thousand of them in *The North American Indian* — are among the most unusual aspects of his achievement, and are certainly the most accessible, so it is not surprising that they should have been the first to find renewed public attention.

They emerged from the limbo of rare book rooms and private collections at a time when present-day Americans were beginning to reap the whirlwind sown during the white man's devastation of the North American continent. It was a time in which we began to reevaluate our cultural ethos and its manifestations in our relationship to the land. The operative equations were becoming clearer as we began to see, and to pay, the price exacted by the natural order of things for our substitution of corporate law for social ethics. Under a president who ruled as a despot, corrupted his office and resigned amidst scandal and disgrace, we found ourselves in a state of advanced political and moral degeneration, alienated from our leadership and ourselves, enmeshed in a seemingly unalterable destructive frenzy aimed at the very earth on which we stand.

It was — and still is — a time for reexamining our fundamental definitions, learning the lessons of history (so as to avoid the doom of repeating it), and questioning our myths. For the first time, contemporary Americans began to face the fact that they lived on land stolen from people who, in their comprehension of man's place in nature and the symbiosis between the two, were infinitely wiser and more mature than those who had seized this country from them. It was becoming more and more apparent that if there were ignorant savages in America's history, they were the ones presently inhabiting and inexorably destroying it.

So we began looking back to those who preceded us here, searching through such fragments as were left for clues to their genius for living in harmony with their environment, a harmony poles apart from this dissonance of ours whose volume mounts daily towards unbearability. The fragments are few, tragically so compared to the totality which once existed. But this extinguished culture's snuffing out had taken place concurrently with the invention of a new and unique graphic medium: photography. Among those fragments, therefore, were images of a new kind, images capable of making the viewer feel and believe that he was looking at reality, at the thing itself and not just a representation of it.

There were hundreds of thousands of photographs of Indian life, and though many of them have not survived the passage of time a large number still exist. Most were taken by photographers who stood as tourists in relation to the Indians; their true subject was their own alienation, and their images are often little more than concretized gawkings. They ascribed no importance to the rhythms, rituals, and symbols of Indian life, and made no attempt to understand and describe these in their photographs. Consequently, their images testify to the gulf between white and Indian culture but provide little insight into the latter, conveying nothing of the feel, tone, and texture of the Indian way of being.

The photographs of Edward Curtis are unique in that they consistently succeed in bridging that gulf between the two worlds. His success is not merely a statistical inevitability, nor the result of luck. Luck plays its role in every enterprise; but, as has been said before, it comes most frequently to those who prepare the ground for it. For all his romanticism (as evidenced by a dashing self-portrait), Curtis was not just an adventurer with a camera, and it was hardly chance alone which brought him the influential support of President Theodore Roosevelt and the financial backing of J. Pierpont Morgan. When, in 1906, those two men respectively endorsed and sponsored the project which ultimately flowered into *The North American Indian,* its originator had been photographing for more than twenty years and studying the

Indians for over a decade.

By the time Curtis began his project the Indians had already been photographed by a great many people, some of them no less gifted than he as image-makers. Curtis, however, far more than they, had developed two aspects of his photography which were specifically valuable and pertinent to the task at hand. One of these is portraiture, which might be termed the craft of particularization. Curtis became a master portraitist, a fact demonstrated time and again throughout this book. His remarkable awareness and use of natural light indoors — the conditions under which most of his portraits were made — is especially significant, not only because it required of him a virtuosic technical expertise but because it granted him the fullest possible control over light as a sculptural tool. This allowed him to model each face he contemplated in such a way as to emphasize its bearer's identity and character. These images bring us close to their subjects as individual beings who confront us, make eye contact with us, demand our acknowledgement of their presence.

Curtis's second strength is his flair for the directorial mode of photography and his genius for what must be called the *mise en image*. All of his tableaux — such as "Start of a War-Party," on p. 31, and "The Parley," on p. 30— were carefully planned; many were actually made during staged reenactments of important ceremonies and historic events. Yet they all have an ease, a sweep and movement astonishing for their day and still effective in ours. There is no stilted acting here, no awkward self-conscious posing, no sense ever that we are seeing anything but the natural flow of events. These images do not merely reflect optical "reality"; they distill each scene, bring it alive, and draw us into it.

Until Curtis, no photographer of the Indians had explored these two areas so thoroughly. Perhaps that is because they were simply photographers, and for them the Indians were no less exotic a visual phenomenon than, say, the geysers at Yellowstone, and not much different in kind when it came to taking their pictures. Particularizing members of a different culture, communicating understandings of their way of life, and creating access to their world are all difficult tasks, calling for abilities which do not develop automatically alongside photographic craftsmanship. Such abilities are based on other forms of knowledge, falling into that field of inquiry we call ethnography, which Webster's defines as "descriptive anthropology."

Edward Curtis may have been an artist, and his photographs may be works of art, but he was by no means an "art photographer." In commitment and in intent, Curtis was an ethnographer devoted to a long-term scrutiny of another culture, who used photography with special brilliance but only as one of many tools and methods available to him for his work.

The impact of his photographs is such that little attention has been paid to the full context in which he placed that imagery, much as a jeweler might set his gems. This book you are holding represents the first real opportunity for members of Curtis's new, expanded audience to experience him fully, not just as a hugely gifted photographer but as a dedicated ethnographer.

Upon its completion in 1930, *The North American Indian* comprised twenty volumes of illustrated text, each accompanied by an additional portfolio of larger, unbound plates. This study of the Sioux and Apsaroke is one such volume, with the text here somewhat abridged and the illustrations combining selections from the best of both the bound and unbound plates.

As such it is representative of the whole, and from it we can learn much — about the Sioux and Apsaroke and about Edward Curtis. We can see that his interest in these tribes was wide-ranging: everything from tipi construction to mythology is observed, annotated, transcribed, and discussed in these pages. Curtis informs us about dietary habits, physical characteristics, hunting procedures, religious rituals — in short, the full span of tribal activity, from the mundane to the exalted. Though he is on occasion patronizing, he manages by and large to convey his perceptions without evaluating or moralizing. His sympathy for the Indians' plight is patent, as is his empathy with the Indian ethos; he appears to have shared with them a common ground of romanticism, which left him perhaps more open to the Indian vision of the universe than some of his more scientifically detached peers.

This empathy, along with the diversity of information he sought out and absorbed in the process of creating his masterwork, are obvious components in his ultimate success. They also contribute to the power and durability of his imagery, for by the time Curtis photographed anything — whether an artifact, a ceremony, a working method or a human being — he not only knew exactly what it was but also its history, its symbology, and its place in the gestalt of tribal life. Images made after such preparation are almost inevitably superior to those made in ignorance, when the purpose is the communicative description of specific perceptions.

There are other traits, too, which visibly nourish both Curtis's writing and his image-making. In both he gives ample evidence of his eye for significant detail, yet never lets it so overwhelm him as to diffuse his larger narratives. He is not only an admirer of story-tellers but an able one himself, with a sense of structure and drama which stand him in good stead photographically.

At the time Curtis initiated his life's work, photography as an adjunct to ethnography was still in its infancy — so, indeed, was the very medium of photography itself. As a photographer, Curtis's accomplishment was the creation of a unified, extensive body of beautifully made images which are strong and direct descriptions of his experiencing of Indian life. As an ethnographer, his achievement was the creation of an irrefutable argument-by-demonstration that the camera was not only useful to ethnography but as indispensable as pen and paper to the full exploration and interpretation of other cultures. Those were no mean feats. Even today, seventy years after Curtis began *The North American Indian* and more than twenty years after his death, there is hardly anything in either field to match it.

A. D. Coleman

Staten Island, N.Y.
December 1974

xvi

We are living in an ultrasophisticated, technologically oriented age. Our lives depend solely on the upkeep of machines. We have been moving in a direction counter to nature in the past few hundred years and have become alienated from the basic elements that sustain life on earth.

The time is now, in a world of hunger, poverty, and political deceit, to reevaluate our basic ethics. The North American Indian lived his life close to nature. It is in nature that we must depend for our survival. Nature holds man's fate.

Edward S. Curtis spent thirty-seven years of his life photographing and recording with camera and pen the life of the North American Indian. Only now, almost half a century after the completion of his project, is his work being realized. E. S. Curtis's *The North America Indian* is a limited edition, collection of five hundred sets, struck from his copper plates. It will always remain in the hands of the few. I do not believe, from reading Curtis's personal notes, that this was his vision. His purpose was to preserve a vanishing race. His intent was for the world to focus on the work *The North American Indian.* In his life, Curtis never saw his vision realized.

Because of my strong affinity for Edward S. Curtis and the mystery attached to the work, I have been inspired to edit *The North American Indian.* I pray that this book will expose the essence of *The North American Indian* and of the remarkable Edward S. Curtis.

Stuart Zoll

Woodstock, New York
February 1975

SHOT IN THE HAND – APSAROKE

INTRODUCTION

In gathering the lore of the Indian of the plains one hears only of yesterday. His thoughts are of the past; to-day is but a living death, and his very being is permeated with the hopelessness of to-morrow. If the narrator be an ancient nearing the end of his days, he lives and relives the life when his tribe as a tribe flourished, the time when his people were truly monarchs of all they surveyed, when teeming buffalo supplied their every want; and his wish is ever that he might have passed away ere he knew the beggary of to-day. The younger man, if a true Indian, is a living regret that he is not of the time when to be an Indian was to be a man.

Strong sympathy for the Indian cannot blind one to the fact that the change that has come is a necessity created by the expansion of the white population. Nor does the fact that civilization demands the abandonment of aboriginal habits lessen one's sympathy or alter one's realization that for once at least Nature's laws have been the indirect cause of a grievous wrong. That the inevitable transformation of the Indian life has been made many-fold harder by the white man's cupidity, there is no question.

Those who do not comprehend the limitations of primitive people protest, "Why sympathize with the Indians? They now have every opportunity that civilized man has, and more, for the Government grants them lands and renders them aid in many ways." The question might as well be asked, why the man born without eyes does not see. The Indian is an Indian not alone in name and in the pigmentation of his skin or his other physical characteristics. He developed gradually and through ages to meet the conditions of a harsh environment exceedingly well, but these conditions were so vastly different from those we have thrust upon him that to expect him to become adjusted to the new requirements in a generation or two would be much like expecting of a child the proficiency of ripe manhood.

Perhaps among no tribe has the encroachment of civilization wrought greater change than among the Sioux, or Dakota. A proud, aggressive people, they depended wholly on the chase and the indigenous vegetation. Powerful in numbers and vigorous in spirit, they roamed almost at will. But in brief time all was altered. The game had vanished; under treaty stipulations which the Indians ill understood they were concentrated on reservations beyond the boundaries of which they must not wander, and became dependents of the Nation, to be fed and clothed according to our interpretation of the compact.

Of the present condition of the Sioux little that is encouraging can be said. They have small hope for the future, and a people without the courage of hope are indeed a serious problem with which to deal. In a few years will have passed away all who knew the old life when means of subsistence were near at hand and the limitless plains were theirs to roam. The younger generation, having no tribal past, may strive to carve a future, and their children, with even less of the instinct of the hunter, will make even better advance; but standing in the way of the present generation and of all the generations to come is the fact that they are Indians, and lack by many ages that which is necessary to enable them to meet the competition of the Caucasian race.

Brought suddenly in contact with the diseases of civilization, the blood of the Indian was particularly susceptible, and the change in food, and in mode of life generally, lessened his vigor and made it the more difficult to combat disease of any sort. In the mixed-blood element must be seen the greatest hope. The proportion of the pure bloods is steadily decreasing, and with each blending the handicap is lightened. The first generation of the amalgamation is on the whole discouraging, but succeeding ones will doubtless show a relatively rapid gain. Even in the West the stigma attached to the possession of Indian blood will gradually disappear, and this in itself will be a factor in the uplifting.

The great change that now comes to the Sioux and to other tribes of the plains with the opening of their reservations to settlement and in the consequent increased contact with alien influences will, within the present generation, further demoralize and degenerate. This, however, is one of the stages through which from the beginning the Indians were destined to pass. Those who cannot withstand these trying days of the metamorphosis must succumb, and on the other side of the depressing period will emerge the few sturdy survivors.

In gathering the material from which this condensed text is selected, the Ogalala, Brule, Miniconjou, Two Kettle, Sans Arc, Hunkpapa, Blackfoot or Sihasapa, and Yanktonai tribes or bands of the Dakota, and their ethnically close relatives, the Assiniboin, were visited by my assistants and myself. The first studies were made in 1905, the final researches in 1907 and 1908. It is to be regretted that it was not feasible to study the Santee Sioux before finishing the investigations summarized in the present volume; but even had this been possible, the desire to extend the comparative work would have persisted. In order to carry out the original plan, the study for each part of the work must not be unduly delayed for further investigation; consequently the publication of the Teton material is not withheld pending the prosecution of field research among the eastern Sioux.

In collecting and arranging the ethnographic material in this volume I have had the assistance of Mr. W. E. Myers. Professor Edmond S. Meany has rendered special aid in compiling the historical data, and Mr. Edgar Fischer has transcribed the music both from his personal field notes and from phonographic records made by other members of my party. Mr. A. F. Muhr has continued his valued services in the laboratory.

Edward S. Curtis

THE SIOUX

PLENTY COUPS – APSAROKE

CRAZY THUNDER - OGALALA

BLACK EAGLE – ASSINIBOIN

THE SIOUX
General Description

The Lakota, or Teton Sioux, during early historic times occupied the region about Big Stone lake, in western Minnesota, whence they moved gradually westward, driving the Omaha to the southward and themselves occupying the valleys of the Big Sioux and the James in South Dakota. Making their way still westward, they reached the Missouri, forcing the Arikara southward and penetrating as far as the Black Hills, so that within the more recent historical period they have held as their home-land the region west of the Missouri river and north of the Platte, extending permanently as far west as the Black Hills, and on the upper Missouri sending occasional parties as far west as central Montana, where the country of the Blackfeet was met. Along the northern line of Wyoming they attempted to take up their abode even beyond the Bighorn. This, however, was the land claimed and held by the Apsaroke, or Crows, who, notwithstanding their inferior numbers, more than held their own and forced the Lakota to the east of Powder river.

In the light of the considerable body of information gathered from the several bands of the Teton it can be safely said that the final or permanent crossing of the Missouri river began from one hundred and seventy-five to two hundred years ago, or between about 1700 and 1725, although previous to this parties had crossed the stream from time to time on hunting expeditions. As to their habitat before the passing of the Missouri, folk-tales, fragments of tradition, and many winter-counts enable us to trace them with certainty back to Mille Lac, Minnesota, in which locality they were found by Hennepin in 1680; beyond this point tradition grows more vague, yet it affords enough of definiteness to entice one to conjecture. "Big Water," of course, could have been the Great Lakes, but according to some of the old men that water was "bitter." Large shells that could have come only from the sea are mentioned. The argument may reasonably be made that these could have been obtained by barter; but the Indians insist that their source was the water beside which their people lived.

No tribe which the writer has studied is so lacking in traditional knowledge of its original home and early migration. In fact, no creation and early migration legend worthy of the name has been found to exist among any of the western Sioux tribes. On the other hand, other tribes of Siouan stock, the Apsaroke, Hidatsa, and Mandan, have definite creation and migration stories, which make it clearly evident that at one time they had their home on the South Atlantic seaboard, where Siouan tribes are known to have lived well within the eighteenth century, and where indeed the remnant of the Catawba still survives. If it can be admitted that the Apsaroke, Mandan, and Hidatsa migrated from the South, it is safe to assume that the plains Sioux came from the same general locality. Sioux tradition, borne out by that of other tribes and by knowledge of their earliest history, is convincing that in their western migration the Sioux passed north of the Great Lakes. This being so, and their origin on the South Atlantic being traditionally clear, their migration has been an exceedingly long one, probably following the line of the Atlantic coast. The very length of their journeying may reasonably account for the lack of a definite migration tradition.

The Hidatsa legend of the creation tells of a land where the birds always sang and the trees were always green. Thence the people moved slowly northward, passing into a land of ever-increasing cold, until they came to a large lake where they found a tribe speaking a language much like their own. They declared: "These people must be our brothers; henceforth we will live together." Feeling that the winters were too rigorous, they journeyed south-

6

westward and southward until they reached the Missouri, where they found the Mandan, who had been living there a long time. This was before the Sioux made their appearance. The probable route of the Hidatsa and Mandan was far shorter than any possible one the Sioux could have taken, and the fact of their slow movement and their long residence in fixed places may well account for the early traditions of these two historically sedentary tribes.

Inasmuch as the Teton, as their name (Titonwan) indicates, have been prairie dwellers for centuries, they must be considered as such, disregarding their earlier forest life. It would seem to be without doubt that the vast herds of buffalo were the cause of their westward movement. Their life was so closely associated with the bison that with the disappearance of the herds the Teton were left pitiably helpless. For generations they had depended in great measure on the buffalo for food, clothing, shelter, implements, and utensils, and because of its necessity in supplying these physical needs it became also a factor of surpassing importance in the religious life of the tribes. Their divine teachings were brought them by a sacred buffalo cow acting as a messenger from the Mystery. In every ceremony the bison played a part, and its flesh was invariably used in the rituals of their worship. But, alas for their religion as well as for their temporal needs, the herds were swept from the earth as in a twinkling. So sudden was the disappearance that the Sioux regard their passing as *wakan,* mysterious. The old men still ask what became of them, and nothing can convince them that the herds have passed forever.

It is doubtful if in the history of the world any people ever were brought so suddenly to such a radical change in their manner of living. The enforced change in diet alone so undermined them physically that they became an easy prey to every ill, particularly the diseases introduced by the white man. Their dwellings became changed from the warm but well-ventilated portable tipis of skins to flimsy ones of cotton cloth, or, worse yet, to small, close, ill-ventilated, permanent log cabins, the floors of which soon reeked with disease-producing filth; their comfortable robes of the buffalo dressed with the hair on were superseded by trade blankets, and unsuitable cast-off garments thrown at them by kindly disposed people. One day they were a proud, care-free people with every desire of the heart to be gratified by slight exertion — the next they were paupers, "wards of the Nation" we call them. From the primitive man's point of view the old life was an ideal one: it gave the Indian every necessity of life with a minimum of effort. His principal labor was that of the chase, which in itself was a pleasure; and on the warrior's return from hunt or raid, the women of the household waited on him as though he were indeed a lord. Even the thought of wasting old age was spared him, for the man whose life was the war-path and the wildest of hunting knew full well that a quick death was apt to be his; and he preferred it thus, insisting that it were better to die while yet strong and happy and when friends' hearts were good, than to grow old and be supplanted by another.

LIFE OF THE WOMEN

Nor was the life of the women the one of drudgery so often depicted. It is true they did the menial work of the camp, but, strange as it may seem, the task was usually a pleasure rather than a hardship, and it is difficult to imagine how, in their stage of culture, the work of the Indians could have been more equitably divided. Owing to the perilous existence of the men and the consequent high deathrate, polygyny was a necessary institution, causing several women to share the burdens of the domestic establishment, and thus lightening the labor of all. Physically the women are equal to any task, however hard. Observed at work, they seem even stronger than the men. In civilization many generations of safeguarding and protecting women have created what we term the "weaker sex"; but among the hunting tribes especially the life of the women has been such as to develop the greatest physical strength, resulting in slight differentiation in features or in endurance of the sexes.

The natural disposition of the Lakota woman is sunny and full of cheer, particularly when she is seen in the home and with her children, where merriment is the normal condition; but when strangers are present the Indian code

8

FLATHEAD WOMAN – APSAROKE

SLOW BULL'S WIFE

of ethics decrees that the woman should be retiring in manner. To her husband she is noticeably affectionate and attentive, waiting upon him constantly, seeing that every article of apparel is brought to him as needed, often literally dressing him as she would a child, and as each article is fastened about her lord's body, she gives it an affectionate pat to show her pleasure in the task. And, indeed, why should she not derive pleasure from such personal attentions? Has she not with her own hands made every article of his apparel — dressed the skins, dyed and fashioned them into form, and with infinite patience embroidered them in beautiful designs with colored quills or beads? And with every stitch there has gone into the work her affection for the man who is to wear the garment, and gentle smiles play about her mouth as she dreams of how proud and fine he will look in his beautiful trappings.

A SEMI-NOMADIC PEOPLE

The Sioux were a semi-nomadic people. Through the summer months they moved their camps to follow the buffalo herds, and day after day the hunting parties went out to the killing. Great stores of the meat were cut into thin strips, dried, and pounded into pemmican for use during the winter months when they could not hunt and kill at pleasure. As the autumn closed and the cold northern winds began to sweep across the plains, the hunting parties, large and small, sought the valley of some wood-girt stream, and there in the protection of the forest remained until spring approached. Robes and furs had been brought in for winter bedding and clothing, and were heaped about the tipis in prodigal profusion. Sufficient jerked meat and pemmican had been provided to last them through the winter months, and these, with the stores of berries and roots gathered and prepared by the women, gave promise of a season of plenty. Occasionally a herd of buffalo came within striking distance and gave the men an opportunity for a grand winter hunt. The meat obtained at this season could be kept fresh until warm weather again approached.

THE BUFFALO CHASE

The buffalo chase, were the occasion winter or summer, was not a matter to be lightly considered; indeed it was a tribal function to be attended with much ceremony. The Sioux, like other Indians, are exceedingly devout, all acts of their lives being attended with religious practices. This was particularly so of buffalo hunting. No individual was allowed to hunt on his own account, for to do so might alarm the herd, and such indiscretion was visited with serious punishment, even with death. After much prayer and many songs, scouts were sent out to look for the game, and during their absence the supplication was continued that they might be successful. When approaching the camp on their return, whether they had been absent a day or a week, the scouts made signs indicating success or failure. Beyond such signals they held no communication with their tribesmen, but made their report to the priests who had performed the ceremonies at the time of their departure. The report was received ceremoniously, and if buffalo had been sighted the crier announced the fact to the entire camp and made known the plans for the hunt. The hunting party was under the leadership of the chiefs, and straggling or individual movement was guarded against by the Soldier Band, the scouts being kept in advance; and if a night camp was necessary, there was more making of medicine that many buffalo might be killed. On approaching the bison the party was kept in a compact body by the Soldiers, that no one might make an impatient start, and at a signal from the chief began their wild sweep down on the stupid but fleet-footed herd.

If a hunting party was so fortunate as to kill a white buffalo, it was an event of great tribal importance. A Ghost Keeper priest was sent for, who first offered many prayers to the Great Mystery, thanking him for this favor, after which he carefully took the skin from the dead animal. No one else was allowed to do this; in fact a white buffalo-skin was holy, and no ordinary man would dare to touch it. The skin having been removed, a horse was brought to convey the *wakan* hide to the village. Sage was placed on the rider's lap

12

that the sacred skin might not be profaned by contact with his body. He took
it carefully to the camp, where it was intrusted to a virgin, who had been appointed to dress it, and who purified her hands in sage smoke before beginning
her task under the direction of a priest of the *Hunka*. After having been carefully prepared, the skin was given over to the keeper of the Calf Pipe, who,
before taking it into the *wakan-tipi*, purified the air with the incense of burning ground-cedar. In the days to come the sacred skin was kept outside of
the tipi and raised high as a sign to the people. "We do this thing as a remem-
brance to White Buffalo Woman, who brought us the sacred ceremonies,"
they said.

METHOD OF HUNTING BUFFALO

The earliest method of hunting buffalo was by making camp around the
herd, with the tipis pitched close together, side by side; then two young men
with *wakan* bows and arrows ran around the entrapped animals, singing medicine-songs to bring them under a spell, so that the people could close in and
kill large numbers. Following this primitive method, they slaughtered num-
berless bison by driving them into a compound — a stockade-like enclosure,
usually of logs, at the foot of some abrupt or sheer depression, its plan of
construction depending on the nature of the ground. In a mountainous region, where the buffalo plains might end at a high cliff, no enclosure was
needed. The long line of stampeded animals would flow over the precipice
like a stream of water, to be crushed to death in their fall. There was no pos-
sibility of drawing back at the brink; the solid mass was irresistibly forced
on by its own momentum, and the slaughter ended only with the passing of
the last animal that had been decoyed or driven into the stampede. At other
times the embankment over which the buffalo ran was only high enough to
form one side of the enclosure. In rare instances pens were built on the open
prairie, and at one side of the stockade was thrown up an inclined approach
along which the buffalo were driven to fall at its end into the corral.

The manner of driving and decoying the bison was as varied as the form of the slaughter-pen; but whatever the method, the purpose and results were the same – the object was to stampede the herd, or a part of it, and to direct the rapidly moving animals to a given point, the Indians knowing that, once well in motion, they would run to their own destruction. The Sioux built out in rapidly diverging lines from the pen a light brush construction, not in truth a fence, as it was only substantial enough to form a line. Men concealed themselves behind this brush, and when the herd was well inside the lines the hunters rose up and by shouting and waving their blankets frightened the animals on. Sometimes a man skilful in the ways of the bison would disguise himself in one of their skins and act as leader of the drove to the extent of starting them in their mad rush. By this method the Indians simply took advantage of a characteristic habit of the buffalo – to follow their leader blindly. The movement grew into a stampede; and forced the leading animals before it. If the advance was toward a sharp gully, it was soon filled with carcasses over which the stream of animals passed; if toward swampy land or a river with quicksand bed, numbers were swallowed in the treacherous depths. If it happened that the route took the herd across a frozen lake or stream, the ice might collapse with their combined weight and drown hundreds; and the Indians relate many instances in which during winter the herd failed to see the edge of an arroyo or a small canon filled with drifted snow and were buried one after another in its depths, the buffalo seemingly not having sufficient instinct of self-preservation to stop or turn aside.

THE EXTERMINATION OF THE BUFFALO

The sportsman and the utilitarian join with the Indians in their cry of regret at the ruthless slaughter of the millions of bison which composed the great western herd, and during the last quarter-century all the harsh language at the command of American writers has been hurled at those directly responsible for the extermination. That the destruction was the most brutal

SIOUX HUNTERS

RED CLOUD - OGALALA

and improvident of its kind in the history of civilization there is no question, and that those who went out and mowed the animals down by scores and hundreds in a single day are deserving of every criticism there is no doubt; but when we view the question in a broader way, the blame would seem to rest not entirely with those who shouldered the guns. It was public sentiment that slaughtered the western herd of the American bison — a sentiment which, fostered by our desire further to oppress, to bring under subjection, and to rob of their birthright a people already driven for two generations before a greedily advancing civilization, was supported by the people as represented in the halls of Congress, and which became the governmental policy. And here lay the blame. We slaughtered the buffalo in order to starve the Indians of the plains into submission, thereby forcing them into a position in which they must take what we saw fit to dole out to them.

In 1871, which might be called the beginning of the last decade of the buffalo, the friends of these animals, and of the Indians, made an effort to promote legislation designed to protect the herds from wanton destruction. In June, 1874, the Senate and the House passed a bill for the protection of the buffalo, but the enactment unfortunately failed to receive the President's signature. During the next four years feeble efforts to the same end were made, but without result. By this time the southern herd was represented only by bleaching bones, while the northern herd was within four years of its extinction. The sentiment of the people at this time is reflected in a contemporary report of the Secretary of the Interior, which says:

"The rapid disappearance of game from the former hunting-grounds must operate largely in favor of our efforts to confine the Indians to smaller areas, and compel them to abandon their nomadic customs, and establish themselves in permanent homes. So long as the game existed in abundance there was little disposition manifested to abandon the chase, even though Government bounty was dispensed in great abundance, affording them ample means of support. When the game shall have disappeared, we shall be well forward in the work in hand. . . .

"I cannot regard the rapid disappearance of the game from its former haunts as a matter prejudicial to our management of the Indians. On the contrary, as they become convinced that they can no longer rely upon the supply of game for their support, they will turn to the more reliable source of subsistence furnished at the agencies, and endeavor to so live that that supply will be regularly dispensed. A few years of cessation from the chase will tend to unfit them for their former mode of life, and they will be the more readily led into new directions, toward industrial pursuits and peaceful habits."

It must be realized that, however comprehensive the legislation and rigorous its enforcement, restrictive laws could only have retarded for a limited time the inevitable extermination of the wild buffalo. If by care they could have been utilized for twenty-five years longer, they would have served, like other things of primeval life, their natural purpose, and we could have viewed their end with only that regret with which we see the forest fall and the prairies' broad surface turned sod by sod from its natural beauty to the utility that Nature's own laws demand.

To have thus husbanded such a vast natural food supply would have been of inestimable value to the white settler, saved untold expenditure in caring for the Indians and many hundreds of them from pitiful starvation, and preserved the virility of the plains tribes. Those, therefore, who feel that the sooner the Indian, like the buffalo, is exterminated the better, must realize that the most effective effort toward this end was the sweeping of the buffalo from the land.

POLITICAL ORGANIZATION

The political organization of the Teton Sioux could not be termed a confederacy. There were seven tribes composing this sub-family — the Ogalala, Brules, Miniconjou, Sans Arcs, Two Kettles, Blackfeet (Sihasapa), and Hunkpapa — and each comprised several smaller groups or bands. Each tribe had a head-chief, *wichashayatapika,* and usually each smaller unit a sub-chief, *itacha.*

In serious warfare these several tribes were apt to form a close alliance for

18

SLOW BULL - OGALALA

LITTLE DOG – BRULE

greater strength, but it was not considered obligatory for any one chief to aid another. Generally, at the inception of a hostile movement of importance, a man of recognized leadership would take the initiative by organizing a war-party, and those who felt so disposed would join him, either as individuals or under the leadership of their own chief. A notable instance is their last great war, which terminated in the victory of the Sioux and their allies over the troops at the battle of the Little Bighorn in 1876. Five of the Teton tribes were strongly represented: the Ogalala, Sans Arcs, Brules, Miniconjou, and Hunkpapa, and these united Sioux tribes were aided by a large party of Cheyenne, while individual members of the other two Teton tribes also joined the hostile forces.

Chiefs were elected at a general council of the men, led by the Short Hair Lodge and similar organizations. Disability by reason of age, or such serious loss of wealth as to make it impossible for a chief to give many feasts or to provide for the poor, were causes for retirement. In the old days the chiefship never descended from father to son, and no man could be elected a chief who had not counted the necessary coups. The council was consulted on questions of public moment, such as laws governing the camp and, particularly, affecting the hunt. Small war-parties were made up without regard to the chiefs or the council, for any individual who could gain a following was free to go against the enemy. General rules were often suggested to the chiefs by the different societies.

THE SOLDIER BAND

Some of the young men, perhaps half of them, were organized into the Soldier Band. When the chiefs met, the Soldiers gathered at the council-place and took their position in front of the tipi, first having gone about the village gathering food for the councillors. The Soldiers, in a way, were the servants of the chiefs, and consequently were supposed to carry out their instructions.

The Soldiers of each village had two leaders, Soldier Chiefs, through whom

21

all commands of the tribal chiefs were communicated to the lodge. When young men were sent out to look for buffalo, Soldiers kept guard so that only those authorized to go could leave the village; and on the return of the scouts with report of where the buffalo were, they assumed charge of the preparations for the hunt, and saw that all started together. Some of the Soldiers remained at home, guarding the village, while others accompanied the huntsmen and kept them together until they had neared the herd. At times in the autumn several bands formed a single buffalo hunting party; on such occasions the Soldiers kept the entire party together, not permitting one band to leave the others until the hunting-grounds were reached, after which the scouts were sent out. When the buffalo were found, the bands hunted together until every one had been supplied with enough meat for the winter. After the general hunt the chiefs gave the command to disband in order that the horses might have sufficient forage, as well as to avoid the sickness which experience taught them followed the practice of camping together in large numbers. This dispersion brought a partial disintegration of the Soldier Band, since each member accompanied his own patriarchal group.

THE LAKOTA GENTILE ORGANIZATION

The Lakota gentile organization has gradually become broken down through general tribal disintegration until little thought is now given to precepts that once were the means of conserving the strength of the blood. Previous to their contact with the white race the laws of the gentes were an important part of their education and were rigidly adhered to. Descent is traced in the male line. The father's brothers are called "fathers," and their children "brothers" and "sisters," as the case may be, while the mother's sisters are addressed as "mothers." The other degrees of relationship have names corresponding to those of our own race. A man on marrying continued to live with his gens. Or he might dwell with that of his wife, but he always retained membership in the gens of his birth, and his children belonged to the

22

same social group. Such a man was called *wicha-woha* ("man buried"). When the wife went to live with her husband's people, she was called *win-woha* ("woman buried"), but she retained her own gens membership. Marriage between members of the same gens was prohibited. A man was not permitted to address directly or to look directly at his mother-in-law or her sisters, but was free to communicate with his wife's sisters and brothers. He dare not speak to his own sister privately, or remain in her company in the absence of others. A wife's brothers were expected to act with diffidence toward the husband's mother and her sisters, but might act with greater freedom toward the husband's sisters. Great respect was exhibited between the daughter-in-law and the husband's father, and between son-in-law and father-in-law. A bond of friendship surpassing even the ties of blood relationship usually existed between brothers-in-law.

Adoption of a son or a daughter to take the place of a child lost by death was common. This was attended by a simple ceremony, consisting of a gathering in a tipi, an address of advice to the new son or daughter by a man chosen for the purpose, and an exchange of gifts between the parents and the parents-to-be.

Wife and husband owned their personal property in severalty. A man dying otherwise than by violence made provision in the presence of his kindred for the distribution of his property among his children, wives, and other near relations. After his death whatever was not thus specifically willed was disposed of by general distribution, and the widow returned with her children to her parents, with whom she lived until another marriage had been effected. Similar disposal was made of the deceased wife's possessions, and in the case of a monogamous marriage the widower returned to his parents and the children were cared for by them or by the wife's parents.

WHEN A CHILD WAS BORN

When a child was born, the parents prepared a feast and sent for a *wichasha-wakan,* asking him to name the infant. The name bestowed was always one suggested by some animal or object seen during one of his fasts, and the accompanying prayer was one taught him during a vision. The Santee custom of giving to children fixed names depending on the order in which they were born did not prevail with the Teton. After a boy had returned from his first war-party he was given an appellation by an uncle or a brother-in-law, and this was later exchanged for a name earned by great deeds. A man could assume his father's name only after having performed acts of such valor as to entitle him to the honor.

At the close of the mother's period of lactation, occurring in two to four years, the parents gave a second feast, when the child's ears were pierced, signifying that the period of abstinence was past and the wife could resume her marital relations. Frequently the piercing of the ears took place during the Sun Dance or other public function. From earliest childhood children were taught in the way that would make them strong and useful members of the tribe. Long before they were large enough to sit unaided on a horse, they were securely tied on the back of a quiet, trusty animal, and there they would sit riding along with the moving band for hours and even days at a time. The boy was early trained to care for horses, driving them in from the ranges to water, and then out again to the grazing lands, and when he had reached his tenth or twelfth year the father usually took him on short hunting trips, instructing him in killing game. The father would drive a young buffalo from the herd, and show the boy how to shoot the animal just behind the shoulder; then followed object-lessons in skinning and dressing. Thereafter he was allowed to single out a calf for himself, and when he had brought it down was made to dress it without help. Even as early as the age of thirteen, seldom later than seventeen, a boy was permitted to accompany his first war-party, and after he had accomplished some worthy deed and thus attained to years of discretion, he was at liberty to marry.

TAKING A WIFE

Having decided upon a girl whom he would make his wife, he places himself by some secluded path where she is likely to pass at nightfall. As she glides with soft fall of moccasined feet along the shadowy trail, the young man slips from his concealment to meet her, shrouded in a sombre blanket, his dark eyes peering out from its folds. The girl may not fancy his attentions and soon pass on, perhaps to meet other suitors. If she be a proud and haughty maiden, several summers may pass with their evenings of courtship ere her heart finally goes out to some favored youth. With her consent to marry, the lovers exchange the marriage-token — a ball of sweet-grass wrapped in deerskin with long fringes to be tied in the hair at the ends of the braids. She then names the time when her lover is to come for her. At this appointed hour he goes to her tipi, cautiously raises the cover at the place where she is sleeping, touches her to apprise her of his presence, when she rises quietly and the two steal forth. The young man then takes his sweetheart at once to his parents' tipi. In the morning the youth's father summons the village crier, bidding him announce that his son has taken a wife, and at the same time a horse is given to some poor person whom the herald publicly names. Thus the two are married. It was never the Teton custom for a young man to take the girl away from the village and live apart with her for a time as a form of honeymoon. Such has occurred in modern times, but only when there was parental opposition to the marriage.

At other times the marriage was of a more conventional nature. The courtship was the same, but the suitor having been accepted and the alliance proving satisfactory to his parents, they sent many presents to the parents of the girl, who, after the family in council had agreed on the fitness of the suitor and the adequacy of the gifts, would signify their consent by making many gifts to the youth's family in turn. If these consisted of horses, the girl was placed upon the finest and was thus borne to the tipi of her lover, where she was received by the women of the family, who spread a large buffalo-robe on the ground for her to step upon in dismounting. Both forms of marriage existed side by side until within recent times. It is, however, self-evident that the latter method was the one followed by daughters of the more important families.

POLYGYNY WAS COMMON

Polygyny was common, the number of wives being limited only by the man's ability to obtain and support them; and the more wives he had the richer he became, as there were that many more workers to prepare skins, which among the Sioux constituted a large part of the wealth. With the consent of his wives a man often married a younger sister of one of them, and usually presents were given for the girl. All lived together in the same tipi, and if a deposed favorite should create discord by reason of her jealousy she was soon sent away. The divorced wife, returning to her parents, married again when the opportunity offered. A runaway wife was more than apt to be killed by the husband, and a meeting between the woman's husband and her new consort was likely to result in a fight with fatal consequences.

MORTUARY RITES

In the mortuary rites of the Lakota the relatives immediately after death combed the hair of the deceased, dressed the body in fine clothing, and painted the face red. Then occurred the first day's performance of the Ghost Keeper ceremony, itself an elaborate mortuary service. After removing a lock of hair, they laid the body on a buffalo robe, wrapped it tightly in several skins, and tied it securely with thongs. For the preparation of the burial-platform, the relatives selected a poor person of the same sex as the deceased, who erected the scaffold in a tree by fastening poles from branch to branch.

26

The same person who prepared the resting-place carried the body out and lashed it securely to the platform. Relatives and friends followed, giving vent to their grief in true primitive fashion by loud wailing and crying. Food was left with the body, and the favorite horse was killed, that the spirit might travel in a fitting manner to the after-world in the south.

An instance of the disposal of the remains of a Sioux warrior killed in battle is related by the Apsaroke. During a clash between war-parties of the two tribes in the Wolf mountains, the Apsaroke were certain that a Lakota, who had ridden a noticeably large sorrel horse, had been killed. They followed the trail of the retreating war-party, and within a few miles of the scene of the fight found the body laid on its tree scaffold. There with painted shield and feather-decked coup-stick proudly hanging above, the warrior lay fastened in the tree, beneath it the body of his favorite horse, which had carried its master to the end of his trail and there been shot that their spirits might journey together.

Burial tipis were sometimes used, a notable instance being the tipi of the dead in the valley of the Little Bighorn, in which, after the Custer fight, were laid side by side, as if asleep, the bodies of some of the fallen Sioux.

MYSTERY POWER

The entire culture of the Sioux is based primarily on two concepts, first, that his "medicine," or supernatural occult power, is derived from the mysterious forces of nature, and secondly, his creed of a brave heart. The conduct and the effort of every Sioux throughout life were so to strengthen his supernatural power that he could not only resist any harm threatening him from ordinary sources, but could become possessed of invulnerability to those imbued with like power. He desired this mystery-power to be stronger than any he was to encounter. Many a brave warrior has cried out to his people that his "medicine" was so great that no arrow or bullet from the enemy could harm him, and, singing his medicine-songs, has charged recklessly into

27

the camp of the enemy and struck them right and left; and, strangely enough, they seem often to have proved their pretension to supernatural strength in that while they were shot at repeatedly at close range they escaped unharmed.

In spite of this strong belief in a tutelary spirit the Sioux was a fatalist, a firm believer in predestination, convinced that if it were so decreed he would lose his life; no subtle power, however strong, no care on his part, could save him. It was his belief further that the spirit or mystery-strength of the animal that appeared to him in vision entered his body and became a part of his *wakan* strength. He might fast many times and have many such tutelary spirits within his body.

WAR SHIELD

Notwithstanding the mystery-power residing within him, the Sioux warrior prepared his war-shield for utility, after which it was consecrated and made *wakan* by painting on it, literally or symbolically, the animals or objects that constituted his "medicine." If it was a bird that appeared to him, feathers of that bird were fastened around the edge of the shield, and as a further protection he wore about his person a portion of the bird; or if an animal, some portion of it, as, for instance, a necklace of bear-claws, was used as a part of the warrior's personal adornment. Ordinarily such objects would be classed as fetishes or talismans, but as used by the Indian they are more than that. Consecrated weapons also formed a part of his war equipment.

COUPS

Coups, or honors, claimed by warriors show to what extent braveness of heart entered into every thought of their life. In camp the chiefs and warriors would meet around the council-fire and recount stories of the war-path, and as each deed was related without challenge, a stick from the bundle kept by the chief would be laid before him. The French-Canadian word *coup,* of such common usage in speaking of Indian deeds of valor, has not been adopted by the Sioux; their term is *toka-kte* ("kill enemy").

A coup could be won by actually killing an enemy, by striking the body of an enemy whether dead or alive, by capturing a horse or a band or horses, or by taking a scalp. Honors were counted on each hostile warrior by the first four who struck him, the first in each case winning the greatest renown, an honor called *tanyan-kte* ("kill right"). Thus, if twenty men were struck or even touched in an encounter, twenty honors of the first grade were won by the victors. But the greatest exploit of all was to ride into the midst of the enemy and strike a warrior in action without attempting to wound him. When a man had led four war-parties, and in each achieved a first honor, he was eligible to chieftainship. If in addition to the recognized coups a man had been wounded, or had had his horse killed or wounded, or had been sent out with a scouting party, he was considered an accomplished warrior and was entitled to wear a scalp-shirt, on which his exploits were indicated by various insignia: a wound was represented by a breast-feather of the eagle, dyed red; a white one signified that the wearer had been a member of a scouting party, while a yellow one denoted a captured horse; and each tuft of the human hair that gave the shirt its name indicated a coup. An eagle's tail-feather was usually worn in the hair for each honor counted. Wounds to man or horse were indicated by marks painted on the body over the injured spot. A man who had killed the first enemy in a battle also painted his face black.

THE PARLEY

START OF A WAR-PARTY

APSAROKE MOTHER

DOES EVERYTHING – APSAROKE

BIRD ON THE GROUND — APSAROKE

THE TIPI

The typical habitation of the Sioux, as of other plains tribes, from earliest tradition to the disappearance of the buffalo, was the skin lodge, in their language *tipi*. The tipi of the old days, when dogs were the beasts of burden, was smaller than during the period following the coming of the horse. The covering was of tanned buffalo-hides, and when new was almost white; but with use and from the smoke of the tipi fire it became a rich brown, and was exceedingly soft and flexible. The skin in this state was called *wizi,* and was much used for leggings and other clothing. To make a small tipi when the dog-travois was the only means of transportation required six or seven hides; but with the broadening of their life by the acquisition of the horse, they made the tipi so much larger that the manufacture of one required fifteen to twenty hides. The tipi-covering was made in sections for convenience in transportation, the strips being fastened together when in place by overlapping the edges and slipping skew-like pins through eyelets. In preparing the hide it was stretched on the ground and firmly fastened with pegs driven through its edge; then with an adze-like tool — made with an elkhorn handle and a blade of steel, and before steel was obtained a piece of elk thigh-bone — the hair was scraped from the hide, which was then flaked down by further scraping to a satisfactory thinness. Spotted Horse Woman said: "I could prepare three hides in a day; that was a hard day's work. Lazy women could not dress so many, and so they had small tipis. My tipi had twenty hides, and it was a fine, big one."

The number of poles required depended on the size of the tipi, twenty-two being necessary for the larger ones. In erecting the tipi four poles were first fastened together near their tops. Two women raised them perpendicularly, and each taking two poles separated their bases until the circumference of the tipi was determined, then the other poles were quickly leaned into place, their bases forming a perfect circle. The sections of skin were next skewered together and the tipi-lifter fastened to the topmost portion of the cover. Now with considerable effort and the assistance of several women the pole with its weight of skins was lifted into place and the covering drawn around the framework. The open ends were fastened together with wooden pins, one woman standing on the shoulders of another in order to reach the highest part of the seam. The bottom was next pinned down and two extra poles were fastened to the outer point of the flaps for use in changing their position when necessary to regulate the draft that carried away the smoke from the fire. A long rawhide rope left hanging from the fastening of the four poles first erected was securely tied to a heavy stake driven into the ground inside the tipi, thus adding to its stability and preventing it from being blown down by severe winds. The lining, a strip of skin extending to about the height of a man, was now attached to the poles inside and fitted securely and closely to the ground, thus leaving an air space between the outer and inner walls. Since the outer covering was not entirely closed at the bottom, perfect ventilation was maintained by means of this air space. In fact for its purpose the skin tipi was an ideal structure — portable, perfect in ventilation, and rigid in wind-storm.

In addition to the tipis used as dwellings there were many that had a public or ceremonious purpose, each with a name indicative of its use. Most striking of these was the *tipi-okihe,* placed at the entrance of the village for use as a guest-house for all visitors to the tribe, and as a public meeting-place, where there was always welcome, and food without asking.

The large dwelling-tipi was very roomy. The family and guests sat or lounged about the edge of the circle, the head of the family or special guest occupying the place of honor at the extreme rear. In winter or during stormy weather all food was prepared over the single fire, and during the waking hours there was a large kettle of steaming food, for a visitor might come at any moment, and failure to offer him refreshment would be regarded as the height of inhospitality.

MAKING CAMP

WINTER – APSAROKE

HANDICRAFT

The handicraft of the Sioux was comparatively simple, the preparation of skins being their most important manufacture. From deerskin they made much of their clothing, as well as pouches, called *pan,* for holding small personal effects; pipe-bags, both *wakan* and for every-day use; saddle blankets for the women; and the carrier for the infant. From the skins of the buffalo were made the tipi-covering, as above mentioned, clothing and blankets, and many durable parfleches of rawhide for carrying heavy articles, as well as food, clothing, and household effects.

Bows were made of ash and cherry backed with sinew. No trace of elkhorn bows could be found. Arrows were pointed with bone, flint, or steel; but flint points have not been made by the Sioux for several generations, probably not since they first crossed the Missouri. On reaching their present habitat they found many stone points scattered about the land; and not knowing who made them they attributed their origin to the supernatural, calling them now "Iktomi arrow-heads," because Iktomi, a legendary hero, is described as having used points of that kind. It has been asserted that the Sioux never made stone arrow-heads, but this statement is difficult to accept, especially since several Sioux tell of having seen their ancestors work stone for this purpose. It is certain that the stone points used by the Teton were practically all found on the ground, having been made, in all probability, by tribes occupying their territory in early times. (Roughly shaped stone hammers, axes, and war-clubs were made; also knives of clamshells bound to wooden handles, and spoons and drinking-cups of mountain-sheep- and buffalo-horn. Bowls were fashioned from natural protuberances on trees, hollowed out by burning and scraping, and highly polished; a carrying bucket was made of the buffalo paunch, with a hoop fastened in the top to hold it in shape. This vessel was used also for boiling food by partly filling with water and dropping therein heated stones. Very large utensils for pounding pemmican and other foods were made of rawhide fashioned into concave form while the skin was fresh.)

The decorative art of the Lakota found expression on their deerskin garments, pipe-bags, saddle-blankets, robes, parfleches, shields, and tipis. Before the coming of traders the designs were worked wholly in dyed porcupine quills; later they obtained beads, which are now used largely, and in a majority of cases the two materials are combined in a single decoration. There seems to be no fixed motif in many of their designs, each woman reading into her art whatever may be prompted by her thoughts, the same figure sometimes meaning as many different things as there are workers.

The Sioux exhibited considerable skill in working red pipestone, or catlinite, into large pipes for ceremonial and common usage. Some were finely inlaid with silver or lead, and in others the bowl and stem were carved in representation of an animal or a bird, the buffalo being the most common subject. While many of the stems were made of pipestone, the majority were of wood, more or less carved, the remainder being beautifully ornamented with porcupine quills or deerskin.

Traditions of the Sioux indicate that they were perhaps the discoverers of the catlinite quarry in Pipestone county, Minnesota, and all such legends and traditions collected by the writer speak of the spot at the time of its discovery as virgin ground, and account for the unusual color by some miracle, rather than describe it as a quarry worked by some mythical people who had mysteriously disappeared — the explanation to be expected if they had discovered old and abandoned workings.

Among the many legends relating to this quarry, which to the Indian is a sacred spot and during historical times has been neutral ground, is one of a battle between the Sioux and the Winnebago. It was of the days when the Sioux were still living on "The Lake" and before they had horses. A brave chief organized a war-party, and, crossing the Great River, they journeyed many days to the southwest, and there in a broad, sweeping prairie valley, broken only by a small stream, were encamped a strong party of the Winnebago. The fight was a long and bitter one, but from the beginning victory seemed to favor the Sioux, and with the closing of the day the last of the

Winnebago had been killed or had escaped — all but a single captive, the beautiful daughter of the Winnebago chieftain, spared by order of the Sioux leader, who would have her for his wife. As he approached the young woman she drew a knife and stabbed herself, exclaiming, "I will die rather than be a wife in the camp of the Sioux!" As her life-blood trickled down in a crimson stream it stained the rock a deep red and thus it has been to this day.

WOMEN'S DRESS

The dress of the women consisted of a garment made of finely tanned deerskins, which extended from the shoulders to midway of the knee and ankle. Sleeves reaching nearly to the wrist were tied at intervals on the under side, ample openings being left at the armpits for the convenience of the mothers in nursing their babes. The sides of the dress were sewn from armpits to bottom. A dress regarded as well-made was fringed at its bottom and sleeves, and finely decorated at the shoulders and arms with porcupine quills, beads, and shells. The one here pictured belonged to a very old woman, wife of the chief Two Strike. It was made by her mother and was worn by herself in the days of her maidenhood, when young warriors were wont to woo her. The little love-charm given her to cast a spell over her youthful suitors is still fastened to the shoulder of the dress.

Leggings extending from knee to foot were worn by the women, and moccasins, ankle-high, usually also beautifully worked with quills and beads. Pendants fashioned from shells were suspended from the ears — often long strings extending nearly to the waist, and each weighing a quarter of a pound or more. Each ear was decorated at times with two strings of ornaments fastened in separate piercings, and massive necklaces made of cylinders of bone were hung about the neck. In winter warm outer moccasins of buffaloskin, with hair inside, were worn, and with a buffalo-robe wrapped closely about the body the Sioux woman was well protected against the severest weather. The hair was parted at the middle from front to back and arranged in two long braids,

41

hanging in front of the shoulders and tied at the ends with a thong and ornaments. In large encampments the lower bodies of the girls were wrapped with deerskin at night-time, that youthful marauders might take no advantage of their heavy sleep of exhaustion entailed by the hard work of the day.

MOSQUITO HAWK – ASSINIBOIN

Ogalala Child

SIOUX MAIDEN

The dress of the men ordinarily consisted of leggings, moccasins, and loin-cloth made from old and soft tipi-covering. The upper part of the body usually was unclothed, but in cold weather was covered with a buffalo-robe held in place by a belt. For ceremonial and dress occasions the apparel of the men was much more elaborate, consisting of deerskin leggings embroidered with quills and beads, moccasins finely stitched and decorated, and in addition to the customary loin-cloth a long strip of embroidered deerskin, eight or ten inches wide, inserted under the belt at the back and permitted to trail the ground. An elaborately ornamented pipe-bag was carried in the hand. The hair in a small circle at the crown of the head was braided and allowed to hang down the back, being tied at the end with a small thong. This was the "top-of-head braid" — what we have come to call the "scalp-lock." From this lock the hair was parted in diverging lines to the temples, and in front was a long bang, kept out of the eyes by wetting and rolling back. The long hair at the sides of the head hung down in two braids wrapped with strips of otter-skin, each with a twisted deerskin thong inside to give it stiffness.

The important article of dress for those who had won the necessary honors to warrant them in wearing it was the scalp- or honor-shirt — a coat-like garment fringed at the bottom as well as along the side-seams and sleeves, and slipped on over the head. In making the scalp-shirt two deerskins of medium size were placed together face to face, sewn at the shoulders, and tied at the sides. The sleeves were sewn firmly at the shoulders and left open along the under side of the arms. The garment was ornamented with bead-work on body and sleeves, and, according to the owner's deeds of valor, with tufts of human hair, weasel-skins, and feathers, each component part of this decoration telling its own story of the wearer's prowess. When taking a scalp, a warrior often removed almost the entire head-covering of the enemy; this was divided into many small pieces for use on the scalp-shirts. The hair of white people was not used for this purpose, as the taking of their scalps was not considered an honor.

The war-bonnet, like the shirt, could be worn only by men who had earned honors in war. When the young warrior had struck the necessary coups, he procured the needed eagle-feathers, took them with suitable presents to some one skilled in fashioning war-bonnets, and asked him to make a head-dress, that he might wear it as evidence of his bravery.

RECKONING TIME

The unit employed in reckoning the passage of time is the winter. There is no name for year, and though there are terms for spring and fall, in general only the two seasons, winter and summer, are recognized. Twelve moons compose the year, for each of which twenty-seven days are marked off on the pipestem; then the moon "dies," and three days are passed before another one rises and the count is resumed. When Ursa Minor is observed in a certain position, the old men say, "The next moon the leaves will be brown." With the new moon, therefore, the tally begins, succeeding moons receiving their appellations from what is regarded as the most striking phenomenon accompanying them. The majority are named from the appearance or habit of the buffalo at the time.

WHITE MAN RUNS HIM

Good Lance – Ogalala

MYTH OF THE WHITE BUFFALO WOMAN

Many generations ago, when the Lakota still dwelt beside the lake far away in the east, they experienced a winter of terrible severity. The snow lay deep on the ground, and the streams were frozen to their very beds. Every day could be heard the sharp crack of trees as the frost gnawed at their hearts; and at night the piles of skins and the blazing fires in the tipis scarcely sufficed to keep the blood coursing through the veins. Game seemed to have deserted the country, for though the hunters often faced the hardships of the winter chase, they returned empty-handed, and the wail of hungry women and children joined with the moan of the forest. When finally a tardy spring arrived, it was decided to leave a country so exposed to the anger of Waziya, Spirit of the North, and seek a better homeland in the direction of the sunset, where ruled the Wing Flappers, who existed from the beginning.

There was little enough to pack besides tipis and fur robes, and what few dogs had not been eaten were soon harnessed to the laden travaux. Two young men were sent in advance. No pair could have been more different in their nature than these two, for while one was brave, chivalrous, unselfish, and kind, the other's heart was bad, and he thought only of the sensuous and vicious.

Unencumbered as they were, the scouts were soon far ahead of the wearily dragging line of haggard men, women bent under burdens that dogs should have been drawing, straggling children, and a few gaunt dogs tugging at the overladen travaux. Late in the day the scouts succeeded in shooting a deer, and thinking their people would reach that point for the night's camp, they left it where it had fallen and were turning away to seek other game when one of them felt a sudden impulse to look back. Wonderful sight! There in a mist that rose above a little hill appeared the outline of a woman. As they gazed in astonishment, the cloud slowly lifted, and the young men saw that she was a

ELK HEAD, AND THE SACRED PIPE BUNDLE

HOLDS THE EAGLE – HIDATSA

Incense over a Medicine Bundle – Hidatsa

maiden far and beautiful. Her only dress was a short skirt, wristlets, and anklets, all of sage. In the crook of her left arm she carried a bundle wrapped closely in a red buffalo-skin; on her back was a quiver, and in her left hand she held a bunch of herbs. Straightway the young man whose heart was evil was overpowered by a desire to possess the beautiful woman, but his companion endeavored to dissuade him with the caution that she might be *wakan,* and a messenger from the Great Mystery.

"No, no!" he cried vehemently, "she is not holy, but a woman, human like ourselves, and I will have her!"

Without waiting he ran toward the woman, who forthwith warned him that she was a sacred being. When he persisted and went closer, she commanded him sternly to stop, for his heart was evil and he was unworthy to come near to the holy things she bore. As he still advanced, she retreated, laid her burden on the ground, and then came toward him. Suddenly it appeared to the waiting youth that the mist descended and enveloped the mysterious woman and his companion. Then followed a fearful sound of rattling and hissing as of thousands of angered rattlesnakes. The terrified observer was about to flee from the dreadful place when the cloud lifted as suddenly as it had descended, disclosing the bleached bones of his former comrade, and the beautiful virgin standing calmly beside them. She spoke to him gently, bidding him have no fear, for he was chosen to be priest of his nation.

"I have many things to impart to your people," she said. "Go now to the place where they are encamped, and bid them prepare for my coming. Build a great circle of green boughs, leaving an opening at the east. In the centre erect a council tipi, and over the ground inside spread sage thickly. In the morning I shall come."

Filled with awe, the young man hastened back and delivered to his people the message of the holy woman. Under his direction her commands were reverently obeyed, for were they not a message from the Great Mystery? In the morning, gathered within the circle of green boughs, they waited in great expectancy, looking for the messenger of the Mystery to enter through the open-

54

ing left at the east. Suddenly, obeying a common impulse, they turned and looked in the opposite direction, and behold! she stood before them.

Entering the tipi with a number of just and upright men selected by the youth whom she had chosen to receive the sacred rites, she at once spread open the red buffalo-skin, exposing its contents — tobacco, the feather of a spotted eagle, the skin of a red-headed woodpecker, a roll of buffalo-hair, a few braids of sweet-grass, and chief of all, a red stone pipe with the carved image of a buffalo calf surmounting its wooden stem. At the same time she explained that the Great Mystery had sent her to reveal to them his laws, and teach them how to worship, that they might become a great and powerful people.

During the four days she remained with them in the tipi she instructed them in the customs they were to observe — how the man who would have great *wakan* power should go into the high places and fast for many days, when he would see visions and obtain strength from the Mysteries; how to punish him of evil heart who sinned against the rights of his brother; how to instruct girls at maturity, and to care for the sick. She taught them also how to worship the Great Mystery by selecting, in the summer of each year, a virgin who should go into the forest and cut down a straight tree; this was to be dragged in and erected for the Sun Dance, but before the ceremony all the virgins should come up and touch the pole, thus proclaiming their purity. But a false declaration would be challenged by the young man who was able to testify to the transgression and she should be driven from the place in derision. A young man wishing success in war or love should paint a rock and make a vow that in the coming dance he would offer himself to the Mystery; then whenever he saw this rock he would be reminded of his vow.

The sacred pipe she gave into the keeping of the chosen young man, with the admonition that its wrapping should be removed only in cases of direst tribal necessity. From the quiver on her back she took six bows and six arrows, and distributed them among as many young men, renowned for their bravery, hospitality, and truthfulness. These weapons she bade them take, after her departure, to the summit of a certain hill, where they would find a herd of six hundred buffalo, all of which they were to kill. In the midst of the herd would be found six men. These also they were to kill, then cut off their ears and attach them to the stem of the sacred pipe. Her last words were these:

"So long as you believe in this pipe and worship the Mystery as I have taught you, so long will you prosper; you will have food in plenty; you will increase and be powerful as a nation. But when you, as a people, cease to reverence the pipe, then will you cease to be a nation."

With these words she left the tipi and went to the opening at the eastern side of the camp-circle. Suddenly she disappeared, and the people, crowding forward to see what had become of her, beheld only a white buffalo cow trotting over the prairie.

THE GREAT MYSTERY

The Sioux, like other Indians, are exceedingly devout in their gropings after deity. They may not be able to explain to alien thinkers their subconscious strength, but their faith is such that almost every action of their lives is formulated by their creed and divine promptings. In their belief the sun, the earth, the moon, the stars, and the more important perceptible forces of nature are personified and deified, and called *wakan,* mysterious. The sun is addressed as *Tonkashila,* Grandfather, and the moon as *Onchi,* Grandmother. In the west is the Nation of the Thunder, the Wing Flappers, who first existed, while from the north comes Waziya, Spirit of the Cold. In extending the pipe in supplication the four cardinal points, the zenith, and the nadir are invariably observed, beginning at the west, but beyond this supplication of the various deities there is the invocation in word and thought of the power that controls all, Wakan-tanka, the Great Mystery. The translation of Wakan-tanka as "Great Mystery" most nearly approximates the true Indian thought, while as rendered for missionary purposes into "Great Spirit" it is misleading, pre-

56

supposing the Lakota to be monotheists, which is far beyond any concept in the minds of the oldest men. Certain men who have been won over to the precepts of the Christian religion translate *wakan* as "spirit," and, attempting to reconcile the primitive with the Christian religion, assert that their people originally believed in a single god. These, however, will quickly break down when confronted with the teachings of their own people.

To the Lakota all things passing the understanding are *wakan*. When supplicating Wakan-tanka, the Indian conceives the Mystery as possessing and being all things that transcend his comprehension. After invoking successively each deity in his belief, he comprehends all in the prayer, "Great Mystery!" and in the cry he has included all the forces of the universe, from that represented by the personal fetish on his body to the undefined consciousness of the infinite.

Not only the heavenly bodies, but cold, heat, snow, rain, frost, a tree struck by lightning — all these, as well as the tipi used for ceremonies and all the consecrated paraphernalia, are *wakan*. The ceremonial pipe is *wakan,* likewise the tobacco-pouch that accompanies it. The spot where the ceremony is held is holy ground, *wakan.* The horse, which came first as a strange, huge beast, they call mysterious dog, *shunka-wakan;* and the gun, which they could not understand, became *maza-wakan,* mysterious iron.

Wakinyan, Thunder, is a nation of enormous birds, the flash of whose eyes is seen in the lightning; of whom, in one of the *Hunka-lowanpi* prayers, it is said, "Ye are half chiefs, half soldiers." Long ago, runs a Lakota tale, a returning party of hunters saw on a bare plain a great white bird, or something in that form. Around it a fog was rising, in the midst of which flashes of lightning were playing. No one dared to approach, but the next day several of the party started back to see what the creature was. Again they found it enveloped in cloud and lightning, and in great fear retreated; but the next day they approached once more. The creature was gone, and where it had lain was now a broad, burned space, from which ran zigzag furrows in four directions. Then they knew that they had seen a Thunderbird.

The medicine practices of the Lakota are inseparable from their religious rites. Disease is evil, brought on by some malign influence, and naturally the treatment is in no case by pharmacy alone. In fact, such medicinal plants as are used are those revealed to the individuals during their fastings, and are therefore *wakan.*

The word "medicine" is continually employed by those writing and speaking of the Indians. This common usage has caused it to appear in modern dictionaries, and, as misleading as the word is, it seems impossible altogether to avoid its use. For this reason it is essential to define its meaning. As used in connection with the Sioux and other plains tribes the word does not in a true sense imply medicinal properties, but rather spiritual strength.

In his *Origin and Growth of Religion* Max Muller discusses *Mana,* a Melanesian name for the Infinite, quoting Mr. R. H. Codrington, a missionary with the Melanesians:

" 'The religion of the Melanesians consists, as far as belief goes, in the persuasion that there is a supernatural power about, belonging to the region of the unseen; and, as far as practice goes, in the use of means of getting this power turned to their own benefit. There is a belief in a force altogether distinct from physical power, which acts in all kinds of ways for good and evil, and which it is of the greatest advantage to possess or control. This is Mana. The word is common, I believe, to the whole Pacific, and people have tried very hard to describe what it is in different regions. I think I know what our people mean by it, and that meaning seems to me to cover all that I hear about it elsewhere. It is a power or influence, not physical, and, in a way, supernatural; but it shows itself in physical force, or in any kind of power or excellence which a man possesses. This Mana is not fixed in anything, and can be conveyed in almost anything; but spirits, whether disembodied souls or supernatural beings, have it, and can impart it; and it essentially belongs to personal beings to originate it, though it may act through the medium of water, or a stone, or a bone. All Melanesian religion, in fact, consists in getting this Mana for one's self, or getting it used for one's benefit.' "

Substituting "medicine" for Mana in the above citation, we have a very satisfactory definition of the term.

A medicine-man is called *wichasha-wakan,* man of mystery. His power is derived from spirits that appear in visions, which he may have in his own tipi as he sleeps at night, or out upon a hilltop whither he has gone for the express purpose of becoming a medicine-man, or in the observance of *Hanbele-cheapi,* the Vision Cry. In his vision a spirit comes to him, sometimes in human form, and commands him to look in certain directions where he will behold *wowash'ake,* power; and there in each place he sees a man standing. As he gazes they vanish, and in their places are certain plants, which he now knows are, for him, medicine. This *pezhuta,* grass-roots, he will use as medicinal remedies, but never are they considered as other than a part of his *wakan* strength. When the dreamer or faster turns about after beholding these powers, he finds that his visitor has vanished, so far as human form goes, and is walking away in the shape of some animal — a buffalo, perhaps, or an elk, or a bear. From the animal he receives certain prayers and songs, which will always remain the same in different ceremonies. The songs and prayers of two medicine-men taught by the same animal vary somewhat, though all bear resemblance to one another. The same man may fast many times, have many visions, and be taught by different spirits; and in addition to his medicine acquired by fasting and supplication he can have transferred to him the medicine-power of others. The medicine ceremony of the Lakota is called *wapiya,* to which is added the name of the animal that taught it, as *Mato-wapiya,* Bear Medicine Ceremony; *Tatankwapiya,* Buffalo Medicine Ceremony.

To illustrate the general custom: A young man has had a vision in which the Bear gave him his medicine. In order to make a public announcement of the fact, he first erects a *wakan-tipi* and calls into it a number of young men, who help him array himself in a bear-skin with the head and claws still attached. Then he comes forth, and word is passed through the village that the bear-man is coming. Men, women, and children scramble hurriedly out of his path, for if he catches one of them he treats him much as a genuine bear would, hugging him and sinking his claws into the flesh of his captive. His young men accompany him, representing bears, though they are not necessarily dressed in skins, and always in advance of the party goes the crier announcing the approach of the bear-man. Henceforth he is known to the tribe as a Medicine-man of the Bear, and he possesses the most efficacious medicine for the treatment of wounds. In treating a patient he first seizes the man by the hair and shakes him, at the same time growling like a bear; then he strikes himself on the sides of his body and spits out several Juneberries, which he picks up and puts in the wounded man's mouth. In his own mouth he places a pinch of the mixture contained in his medicine-pouch and blows it into the mouth of the patient. Then some of it is sprinkled on the man's eyes, rubbed on his temples, and held under his nose for him to inhale. If no improvement is shown, he proceeds no further, for there is no use: the man is bound to die. If, on the other hand, the patient seems to yield to the treatment, the medicine-man continues it by making incense of sweet-grass and purifying in it his *wopiye,* a long rawhide cylinder, three or four inches in diameter, from which he then takes his medicine and puts it into a bowl of water. Next he repeats his own individual prayer, which is addressed to the bear and for the greater part is merely a description of the appearance of the animal that came to him in his vision, ending with a request that he "make his deed powerful." Then he gazes into the bowl, and from the fantastic shapes of living creatures that the mixture, to his imagination, assumes, he predicts recovery. Three of four assistants, men whom he has previously treated for illness, now beat the drum and sing the Bear songs. The medicine-man, while they sing, approaches the patient, simulating the actions of a bear, lifts him and almost throws him down, tumbling him over and over, just as a bear might do. The mixture is then administered, a portion being first blown upon the wound. This treatment is repeated once or twice daily during the four days.

Medicine-men of other animals confine their incantations to one day, following much the same course of procedure, each impersonating the animal from which his power is derived. There is no ceremonial gathering of herbs, the plants revealed in the vision being collected immediately after the public announcement of the fact that one is a medicine-man, and thenceforth as occasion requires. In treating disease the medicine-man locates the seat of the ailment by mixing his medicine in a bowl and obtaining the desired inspiration from some peculiarity of the shape it assumes. The affected spot he then sucks, and spits forth either blood or some sticky substance, ostensibly pus.

Strong light is thrown upon the method of acquiring medicine-power by a description of *Hanbele-cheapi,* the Vision Cry, one of the ceremonies taught by White Buffalo Woman, as previously mentioned. It shows clearly that the men are not mere idle tricksters, as is generally supposed, but rather, within the limits of the primitive mind, thinkers, understanding well the great mental and spiritual power to be gained by subduing the physical man and by concentration of thought.

THE VISION CRY

The father of a child seriously ill may beseech its recovery by a vow to worship the Great Mystery in fasting and prayer. First, filling his ceremonial pipe, he takes the child out under the open sky at break of day, holds it in his arms, and reverently raises the pipe aloft to the west, praying, "Great Mystery, All-powerful, permit this child of mine to recover health, and when the summer comes I will worship you with many offerings." The Vision Cry may also be observed by one desirous simply of a revelation and the gift of mystery-powers. As soon as possible the intending faster collects the materials for the promised offerings: a red-painted buffalo-robe, a calf-skin, tobacco, and kinnikinnick; all of which, wrapped in a bundle, he suspends from the tipi-lifter, where they remain until the time comes to redeem the vow.

Near the end of June he summons to his tipi, through the herald, the prominent men of the village. In silence the pipe is filled and passed about the

61

circle. Soon the host apprises the company of his unredeemed pledge to the Mystery, and inquires if they know of a man who understands this rite. "Yes," is their response; "we know of one who is a priest of this *Hanbele-cheapi.*" At once he fills a pipe, bears it to the tipi of the priest, and silently extends it to him. Without a word it is accepted, lighted, and offered successively to the spirits of the Four Winds, the Sky Father, and the Earth Mother. Having smoked with deliberation, the priest speaks:

"I understand what you wish. This is my rite. I stood alone a day and a night, worshipping the Great Mystery, but it was hard. Do you wish this one day? If you do, tell me. Then I stood two days and two nights alone on a hill. That was yet harder. Do you want that? If you do, tell me. Again I stood three days and three nights, crying to the Mystery, and it was very hard. Do you want that? If you do tell me. Then I stood four days and four nights upon a hilltop, praying and crying to the spirits of Sky and Earth, to *Wakan-tanka,* Great Mysterious One. I drank no water and ate no food. That was the hardest of all. Do you want that? If you do, tell me."

"My heart is strong; my father's heart was strong. I have promised the Great Mystery to worship him. I will fast four days and four nights," is the response.

"It is very hard, but the Mystery will aid you. Go now to your tipi; choose two good young men and request them to build a sweat-lodge for you early in the morning."

The selection of the two *Ini-wowashi,* Sweat Workers, and the bestowal of presents upon them, end the day's preparations.

At sunrise the sweat-lodge is erected, facing the east. In the centre is a small pit to hold the heated stones, and behind this the ground is strewn with sage. Ten paces from the entrance the turf is removed from a spot designed to receive the fire and is heaped up just east of the cleared space. Firewood and twenty-five smooth round stones are gathered, and the latter, painted red by the faster, are thrown into the leaping flames. The priest enters the sweat-lodge, and, sitting in the place of honor at the rear, lays before him the bundle containing red robe, calf-skin, tobacco, and kinnikinnick. These articles he unwraps, while the faster enters and sits down at his left. He next commands the Sweat Workers to procure four young cherry stocks, in length seven or eight feet, untrimmed and not cut with axe or knife, but twisted and broken from the roots. Two buffalo-chips are laid side by side back of the stone-pit, and behind them a glowing ember, carefully borne on the prong of a fire-stick, is deposited by one of the young men. With the never-omitted motions of raising the hand to the four world-quarters, the sky, and the earth, the priest makes sacred smoke by dropping a bit of sweet-grass upon the coal, and passes the tobacco through the incense four times, to make it sacred. Having thoroughly mixed tobacco and kinnikinnick, he sanctifies the pipe by rubbing his hand downward on each of its four sides, before each movement placing the hand on the earth as if to draw its essence from it. Then with ceremonious deliberation he fills the pipe, seals it with buffalo-tallow, ties a stalk of sage about each extremity of the stem, and hands it to the faster, who places it, bowl to the westward, on the heap of turf outside.

The priest is now to prepare *waonyapi,* offerings to the Great Mystery. The principal *waonyapi* consists of a quantity of tobacco tied into a corner of the red robe, which is attached to a branch of one of the cherry poles. For the others fifty smaller portions of tobacco tied up in pieces of calf-skin are fastened to the twigs of the other three boughs. All four are then deposited in a row to the east of the pile of turf, the principal offering being farthest removed. Beyond this is placed a buffalo-robe, previously purified in sacred smoke. During the portion of the ceremony thus far performed — *Wakan-kaghapi* (make sacred) — no one save the two young men is permitted to approach the sweat-lodge, which is *wakan*.

Priest and faster now step outside and remove their clothing, while one of the Sweat Workers calls for worthy men to come and take part in the sweat. Those who respond disrobe to the loincloth and follow the two principal actors into the sudatory. None may touch the faster, for he is holy. When all are seated, the priest chants a song and speaks:

"This is my rite. This young man has given me many presents and asked for *Hanbele-cheapi.* I have worshipped the Great Mystery many times, and I now ask Thunder for a blue day. The Mystery has created many animals, some of which are like men. This young man will see them."

Continuing, he instructs the faster:

"This sweat removes from your body all evil, all touch of woman, and makes you *wakan,* that the spirit of the Great Mystery may come close to you and strengthen you. When our sweat is over, you will take pipe and buffalo-robe and go to some high mountain where the air is pure. On your return you must be careful to speak the truth in telling us of your visions, for should you deceive us, we might work you great harm in trying to aid you in interpreting the revelations sent by the Mystery."

The stones, glowing white with heat, are placed in the pit. The priest offers to the Great Mystery a small piece of dog flesh and another of dried buffalo-meat taken from a bowl of each brought by the faster's relatives, and after marking with charcoal two stripes across the inner surface of a wooden cup, he fills it with water and gives both meat and cup to the faster. The attendants close the entrance, the priest chants another song, and, bidding the faster cry, dashes water twice on the stones. After a time air is admitted; then follows another song, and more water is thrown on the stones. Twice more this is repeated, and the faster, never ceasing to cry aloud, comes forth, puts on his moccasins, takes the pipe in his left and the robe in his right hand, and starts out on his sacred journey. Behind him follow the two *Ini-wowashi* bearing the offerings.

At the foot of some lonely hill miles away from human habitation the faster halts, still crying aloud to the Great Mystery and holding the pipe before him in supplication. The two attendants pass by him and proceed to the summit, where they plant the four *waonyapi* at the corners of a square of some six or eight feet, the chief offering being, of course, to the west. Within this space they spread a thick covering of sage, for this is sacred ground and must not be touched by the feet of the suppliant.

64

The faster is now left alone in the presence of the Mysterious. Reverently he removes moccasins and loin-cloth, throws the robe about his shoulders, and stands with uplifted face in the centre of the sacred square, extending the pipe to the sun. At noon he turns and prays to the Mystery of the South; at sunset to Thunder, the Wing Flapper, Spirit of the West. As darkness spreads over valley, plain, and hilltop, he lies prone, with face still turned to the west, calling upon the Thunder Mystery to grant him a vision. In awe-inspiring solitude and the darkness of midnight he prays to Waziya, who sends the biting north wind and blinding snow, and who also controls in some mysterious way the movement of the buffalo. The first glimmer of dawn beholds him in the attitude of humble supplication before the deity that holds sway in the east. As the rim of the sun appears above the horizon he stands erect, clasping the shaggy buffalo-robe to his breast and offering the pipe to the orb, while with loud cries he expresses to the mysterious powers of the universe his heart's desires.

Having become *wakan*, mysterious, supernatural, by reason of the ceremonial sweat, the faster is now able to understand the speech of supernatural beings, and of animals and birds. At some time during his vigil on the hilltop one of these creatures — bird or beast, tree, rock, natural phenomenon, ghost of ancestor — appears before him, either in its own proper body or in the form of a man, and after commending his strength of heart in having endured the pangs of hunger and thirst and the temptation of evil spirits to leave the sacred spot in fright, the spirit-being reveals to him information of the future, and then, pointing out some shrub or plant, says: "There is medicine; take it, and cure your people of illness." Thus every man who has seen such a vision becomes, to a certain degree, a medicine-man; whether he uses his divinely given rites and remedies so extensively as to be known generally as a dispeller of disease, *wichasha-wakan*, man of mystery, depends upon his own initiative. He has the medicine; it is for him to use it, much or little. The mysterious creature itself becomes the suppliant's tutelary spirit, his so-called "fighting medicine," to aid him in battle and in every crisis of life. Its image is

65

painted upon his shield, his tipi, his gala robe, and before entering upon any undertaking of importance he beseeches its favor and guidance in prayer and song.

But not to every one that endures the pangs of the four days' fast is it given to behold a vision. While to some may be unfolded many events of the future in the course of a single fast, there are many well-known instances of a man having sought more than once in vain for a revelation of the supernatural. The truth of the vision seen is never questioned; it may be wrongly interpreted, but always subsequent events will prove that the spirit-creature was not at fault. It follows naturally that a man never feigns to have seen a vision, for such a course could result only in misleading the people and thus bringing misfortune when the sages give their interpretation.

The first day of the fast is the prototype of those that follow. If in the end the seeker after divine favor is still denied his prayer, he no longer stands with face confidently uplifted to the mysterious powers, but sinks to the ground, bowing his head upon his knees in utter dejection, and praying, aloud or in silence, to the Spirits of the West, the North, the East, the South, the Sky, and the Earth. His eyes are downcast, averted from the face of the Great Mystery in the sky until his appeal is granted and the revelation given, or until he has relinquished all hope, knowing that in some way he has offended the divine ones and that the power of the supernatural, for the present at least, is denied him.

When the proper time has elapsed, the two attendants return to the hill, mounted, and leading a horse for the faster, who, weak and emaciated from hunger, thirst, and lack of sleep, is lifted bodily to the animal's back and supported as the horse is led slowly homeward. The trio halt in front of the sweat-lodge, into which the priest and a helper bear the faster, still clasping his pipe. The old men, anxious to hear the story of his visions, quickly disrobe and enter. The faster can now detect a disagreeable human odor, for he is holy, and human flesh, however clean, has for him a peculiar smell. The priest takes the pipe from his hands, removes the tallow, and, looking into

66

the bowl, says:

"There is nothing in it. What have you done that the pipe is empty?"

"I do not know," answers the faster.

"The Mysteries," solemnly announces the priest, "have smoked this pipe. Tell us, my friend, truthfully all that you have seen."

The vision, if one has been experienced, is then described, and, unless its significance is obvious, is interpreted by the priest and the sages. A cup of water and a piece of meat, both having first been purified by exposure to the incense of sweet-grass and offered to the Mysteries by the priest, are given to the faster, and the sweat now takes place as on the first morning.

On the distant hilltop remain standing the four withered boughs bearing the robe and the little bags of sacred tobacco, offerings to the mysterious, the infinite, the incomprehensible powers of sky and earth.

Ceremonies

THE SUN DANCE

In one form or another the Sun rite was practically universal among the tribes of the Great Plains. The Sioux in all their numerous branches; their cousins, the Assiniboin, Mandan, Hidatsa, and Apsaroke or Crows in the north, the Omaha, Ponca, Kansa, and Osage in the south; the Arapaho, Cheyenne, and Blackfeet; the Arikara, Pawnee, and Wichita; the Ute, Shoshoni, and Kiowa — all did reverence and made supplication to the mysterious power that comes with the morn and disappears with the dying day. Naturally, among such widely separated groups, extending as they did from the Mississippi to the Rockies and from our northern border well-nigh to the Gulf of Mexico, the Sun rite differed not only in the details of its performance, but even in the thought that underlay it. Yet so striking were the similarities in practice and purpose, that, while speculation as to the origin of these rites is futile, one cannot escape the conviction that they all flow from a common source. of the ceremony many others may express the same intention; but the man who first made known his vow is the Chief Dancer.

67

The Sun Dance Votary – Apsaroke

This most characteristic of the religious ceremonies of the Sioux was an occasion of thanksgiving, of propitiation, of supplication for divine power. Participation in the dance was entirely voluntary, a mental vow to worship the Mystery in this manner being expressed by a man ardently desiring the recovery of a sick relative; or surrounded by an enemy with escape apparently impossible; or, it might be, dying of hunger, with helpless children crying for food that he could not supply, since some inscrutable power had swept all game from forest and prairie. Others joined in the ceremony in the hope and firm belief that the Mystery, worshipped with such zeal and with such manifestation of valor would grant them successes against the enemy and consequent eminence at home; while always there was present the idea, perhaps subconscious, that the supernatural, even though a beneficent being, must be propitiated against future anger.

The silent vow of the worshipper, though as binding upon him as any oath, must be supplemented by a public declaration to the Great Mystery himself. At the earliest flush of dawn he rises and fills his ceremonial pipe, and slowly proceeds to the tipi of the village herald. "My friend," he says, "I bring you this pipe. I desire you to announce to the Great Mystery that I wish to worship him." The two smoke in silence, and the votary returns to his own tipi, followed shortly by the other. The herald fills the pipe, steps outside, and with stem extended upward to the west calls long and loud, *"Hanhan-n-n-n!"* Four times thus he strives to gain the ear of the Mystery, and then invokes him:

> "Great Mystery, Grandfather, look this way !
> Wing Flapper, Soldier, Grandfather, behold me !
> This young man will offer you a pipe,
> That before you he may grow and be strong.
> Spirit-creatures of the Four Winds, to you will he extend a pipe;
> A red robe will he raise and bring to you.
> This day let the nation live."

A smoke ends the announcement. In the interval between this and the day

From now on until the summer solstice, when the dance takes place, the life of the votary is dedicated to the purification of body and mind. He is frequently in the sweat-lodge and drinks quantities of various herb decoctions. He is careful to avoid contact with any unclean person or thing. Fighting is not for him, and calm deliberation characterizes all his acts. Much of his time is spent in prayer and in crying aloud to the Mystery.

When the season of the Sun ceremony is at hand, it becomes necessary for the votary to select a medicine-man to preside over the rites. Clad in new moccasins, leggings, and loin-cloth, a thick-haired buffalo-skin thrown over his shoulders, he mounts his horse and, accompanied by a friend similarly garbed and mounted, proceeds, stern-faced and silent, his pipe filled and sealed held ever before him, to the home of the Priest. The horses are not permitted to go faster than at a slow walk, even though the chosen mystery-man live in a village so distant that the entire day is consumed in the journey. During all this time the worshipper must not dismount, and not a drop of water moistens his lips; for this is a part of his sacrifice.

News of his coming has already been conveyed to the medicine-man, who waits in his tipi with his herald. As the Sun Dancer enters and lays his pipe in front of the Priest, the herald calls out the usual formula, *Iyun hahekupo!* "All come home!" a summons to those entitled to sit in council. When the assembly is complete, the medicine-man purifies the pipe in the sacred incense of sweet-grass, and prays, holding forth the stem to the west:

> "O Great Mystery, Grandfather, you will be the first to smoke this pipe.
> Wing Flappers, you in turn will smoke.
> This day may the nation live.
> A blue day you will hold before my face."

Then, beginning at the entrance, he holds the pipe for each one present to smoke, and after an intricate series of ceremonious motions returns it to the suppliant, bidding him remain until morning, when his journey of announcement and invitation to the other villages will begin.

Morning dawns, and the mystery-man fills and seals the pipe and places red paint before the guest, who rubs it on his palms and smears his face and body. "Now, on your way," says the medicine-man, "when you grow thirsty, dismount and drink, for this paint has purified you and made you *wakan*. Therefore you may drink, but not from a vessel; on hands and knees you must drink from the stream."

The Sun Dancer and his attendant resume their journey with the sacred pipe, and, coming into the next village, enter the tipi of the chief, who forthwith summons his old men. A medicine-man sits down beside the chief, and with the words, "It is already prepared," makes offering of his pipe to the Mysteries of the Four Winds, the Sky, and the Earth, then carries it about the impassive circle.

"What did the Priest say to you?" the chief inquires.

"He said they would move to the ground four days thence," answers the Dancer.

"Then we will all move at that time," is the response.

Food and water are placed before them by the chief's wife, and soon the messengers set forth to the other villages.

Two days before the time set for the ceremony to begin the camp of the Chief Dancer moves to the spot selected, where the young men immediately plant green branches two or three yards apart to form a circle perhaps a mile in diameter and open to the east. During this day and the next the bands gather and pitch their tipis in a single large concentric circle outside that of the green boughs. Inside the latter each village erects a tipi for the use of such of its members as are to participate in the rites. Thick branches are piled close around the bottom of the tipi-wall, to prevent the entrance of cool, refreshing air, and in the evening a fire is kept burning. Having once entered their tipi of preparation, the dancers cannot leave it until the actual dancing begins three days later; nor may they scratch the head or body with the fingers, each being provided with a forked stick made for that purpose by one of his relatives. Each dancers' tipi has its attendant, who at sunset on the last day of camp preparation makes ready the sweat-lodge. After a final purification of

71

the body the dancers enter their respective tipis.

A part of this night and of the two succeeding nights is devoted to the Imitation Dance, a rehearsal of the Sun Dance songs. The dancers sit in a circle around the edge of the tipi, the remainder of the space being filled with men of such prominence as to entitle them to participate. A great vessel of cooked dog-meat and buffalo-tongues is supplied by the women, but before food is touched, the songs of the Sun Dance are repeated to the accompaniment of the drums. Only the drummers and four women who sit behind them sing, the dancers retaining their places on the ground, but blowing constantly on their eagle wing-bone whistles. The fire is extinguished before the singing begins, and is relighted at the conclusion of the last song.

The next day is the first of the ceremony, and the scouts who are to search for the Mystery Tree are selected. In the early morning the heralds ride about the camp-circle, the *hochoka,* bidding all men assemble in a chosen spot. There the chiefs select four men, who, dressed in full war regalia, seek out certain noted warriors, men of distinction, their chief a warrior who, while scouting, found the enemy, killed his man, and brough back a scalp with the news. These scouts, six or eight in number, dress and paint as for war, and prepare to search for a tree already marked out by the Chief Dancer's attendant, who, soon after the assembling of the bands, went into the woods and selected a tall, straight cottonwood from eight to twelve inches thick, leaning two poles against it as an indication that it had been chosen for the Mystery Tree. Drums beating and drummers singing, the scouts form in single file and ride four times around the *hochoka,* then away toward the timber, accompanied for a distance by a legion of horsemen dashing around and around them. From the camp comes the song of the drummers, "He has gone again, he has gone again," meaning that the leader of the expedition is once more scouting in the enemy's country. The scouts disappear, and in the direction taken by them, some two hundred yards from the camp, the young warriors set up a bundle of branches to represent the enemy. After a while the absent party reappears, and about half a mile distant halts, while the leader utters the coyote cry; then, single-file, all ride toward the camp in a zigzag line, a signal that they have found the enemy. With one impulse the restless steeds of the impatiently waiting young men leap toward the returning party, sweeping around them four times in a great seething circle. Then back wheels the whole tumultuous horde, thundering down upon the "enemy." War-bonnets stream; weapons are brandished aloft; horses strain eagerly forward. Loud and shrill the war-cry fills the air. For the moment the most ardent wish of every horse-man is to reach the goal first, and no risk of reckless riding is too great to be taken in the effort, for he who is first to strike the bundle of boughs with bow or staff and utter the exultant shout, *"Anhe!"* feels himself assured of achiev-ing an honor of the highest class in his next battle.

Meanwhile the scouts have ridden into camp and dismounted. The chief gives their leader a pipe, and says: "Man, you are acquainted with all the creeks. You have been up and down all of them. If you have seen the move-ment of a coyote, tell me."

The leader answers figuratively: "I have seen a small village of the enemy moving toward us, and on the way back there were many buffalo."

The scouts disband.

In the afternoon the chiefs assemble in the *hochoka,* and the Priest and the Chief Dancer bring two ceremonial pipes, already filled, and present them to the two medicine-men. The one thus chosen by the Priest is to dig a hole for the Mystery Tree, while the other presides at its felling. Each smokes and passes the pipe to the others, signifying his willingness to perform the service requested of him.

Some time during the morning of the second day the medicine-man select-ed by the Chief Dancer fills his ceremonial pipe and sets out for the chosen tree, four chiefs abreast behind him, and a throng of people following them. He sits at the foot of the Mystery Tree and holds his pipe out to it before making a similar offering to the Four Winds, the Sky, and the Earth. He smokes alone. The four chiefs sit in a row at a distance of about fifty yards, and between them and the tree no one may pass. They are now joined by the medicine-man, and two of them summon from the assemblage four warriors of distinction, whom they station in a row beside the tree. Next a virgin is selected and placed beside them. First passing an axe through the smoke of sweet-grass, the medicine-man gives it to one of the warriors, who relates his greatest exploits and strikes one blow at the tree. The other three follow his example, and the girl completes the work. The fall of the tree is greeted with a concerted shout, and the young men rush upon it as if attacking an enemy, striking it with cries of *"Anhe!"* The maiden proceeds to trim the trunk, cutting off a length of about thirty feet and leaving at the top a fork with its branches and twigs.

Some of the men at once place short poles under the Mystery Tree and bear it to camp, stopping four times on the way to give the coyote howl. The fourth start is made at a point about a quarter of a mile from the camp-circle, whence the carriers set out at a trot. Immediately bursts from the edge of the timber a swarm of men and youths, women and girls, the former in another wild charge upon the "enemy," the latter in a more leisurely return to the camp, horses bedecked with branches and trailing vines, and each person bearing at least one green bough to be used in the construction of the dance-lodge.

During the felling of the tree, the other medicine-man, the one chosen by the Priest himself, has been engaged in excavating a hole for it in the centre of the *hochoka,* piling the earth to the west. The carriers enter running and deposit the Mystery Tree on the ground, the butt resting on the heap of fresh earth with its extremity directly over the hole. A sheaf of untrimmed cherry sticks is placed beside the tree near the crotch. This ends the ceremonies of the second day, and a general round of feasting ensues.

The events of the third day centre about the raising of the Mystery Tree. The Priest and the Chief Dancer issue from the dancer's tipi bearing certain ceremonial articles now to be used, and the former ties the sheaf of cherry sticks in the angle of the fork, covering it with an entire buffalo-skin painted red on the inner side. Along the nose of the skin are fastened bunches of eagle-feathers. The medicine-man who superintended the cutting of the tree now holds a piece of buffalo kidney-fat over the hole prepared for the tree, prays silently, and drops the fat therein. The Priest draws four red lines down the length of the pole and suspends from the fork a small rawhide effigy of a man — an enemy — and another of a buffalo. Two deerskin bags hang from the tree; these, as well as the images, are offerings to the sun. Two ropes are now attached to the top, and with men pulling and others lifting, the Mystery Tree is raised slowly and dropped into place amid a deafening shout.

The construction of the dance-lodge is next begun; this is simply a leafy screen supported on two concentric circles of forked sticks, with a wall of leaf shields and vines in which openings are so numerous that spectators can find no cause for complaint. An attendant is now despatched for a dry buffalo-skull, which is placed on a bed of sage west of the tree and is painted by the Priest with stripes of red. After the painting the skull becomes a sacred object whose presence will insure an abundance of buffalo in the ensuing fall.

Meanwhile a number of men have painted their faces white, and donned war-bonnets and scalp-shirts, if they have attained to that dignity. At the cry of the herald these come trooping into the lodge in single file for the performance of the Dance That Smooths The Ground. As the musicians drum and sing, the participants dance toward the pole, shooting at the two rawhide effigies of enemy and life-giving buffalo, retreating and advancing alternately. Both images are soon brought to the ground amid a storm of war-cries. It is now late afternoon, and from the close of this evening's meal the dancers will abstain from food and water until the end of the ceremony.

The final day dawns, but not before the Priest has arisen and purified his body with sacred smoke. Thus prepared, he paints the Chief Dancer with a black semicircle from the forehead down each cheek, others at the shoulder joints, and full circles about elbows and wrists. The rest of the body is painted red; and a roll of buffalo-hair is tied to each elbow and each wrist, to the latter being attached also small pieces of human scalp with long flowing hair. A single eagle-feather is fastened in the hair of the Chief Dancer.

75

At daybreak the participants file into the dance-lodge, where they are painted by the medicine-men. They are clad in double aprons of deerskin from waist to knee, and buffalo-skins, the hairy side outermost, about their shoulders and belted at the waist. From the neck of each is suspended his eagle wing-bone whistle, the mouthpiece wound with sage and the other end adorned with an eagle-feather.

All having been painted, they arise, dropping their buffalo-skins, and the Priest leads in the Chief Dancer, who takes his place in front of the others, all facing the east. Standing behind the Chief Dancer, the Priest points his whistle to the east and blows a shrill note beside the Dancer's right ear, then another at his left, and a third above his head — three invocations to the Mystery of the Sun. The other participants hold right hands outstretched toward the rising orb. Next the Priest leads them successively to the south, to the west, and finally to the north of the Mystery Tree, following the direction of the sun's course and sounding his whistle toward each point. The dancers now station themselves about the enclosure by villages, their leader between the pole and those assembled on the western side. All face the east, and at the word of the Priest, who stands just west of the painted buffalo-skull, the drummers commence to sing and the dancing begins.

As they dance, the performers never leave the spot on which they stand, the movement consisting in a slight upward spring from the toes and ball of the foot; legs and body are rigid. Always the right palm is extended to the yellow glaring sun, and their eyes are fixed on its lower rim. The dancer concentrates his mind, his very self, upon the one thing that he desires, whether it be the acquirement of powerful medicine or only success in the next conflict with the enemy. As the day wears on, this unceasing mental concentration produces that state of spiritual exaltation in which visions are seen and the future is revealed.

Each song is chanted four times, and then follows a very brief interval for the singers to prepare for the next — a moment during which the dancers may rest standing, and lower their eyes to the ground.

76

When the zenith is reached, the Priest fills a pipe and hands it to the Chief Dancer, who proffers it to some individual, himself a former principal actor in the ceremony and therefore familiar with the proper mode of piercing the breasts, the pipe is refused. The Dancer attempts to force it upon him, striving to open his hand and thrust the pipe into it. But the hand is clenched. The Dancer then returns to the Priest, but receives the command, "Go again!" Once more, therefore, the trial is made, and yet again, but each time the pipe is declined. At the fourth offering, however, the pipe is accepted with the words *"Ho!* It is hard, but if you wish it, it shall be done to you;" and the pipe is lighted and smoked. When the Dancer has returned with the empty pipe to his customary station, the man chosen by him secures a picket-pin and splits it into quarters, two of which he reduces somewhat in thickness and to a length of about six inches, making them smooth and triangular. Singing and dancing cease. Over the multitude spreads a hush of expectant emotion, as he places the skewers on the ground beside the Dancer, and standing erect prays:

"Great Mystery, this is I who worships. This thing will I do, though it is hard. This young man requests it, and I will do it for him."

Then spreading sacred sage upon the ground south of the Mystery Tree, he leads the Dancer thither, lifts him bodily in his arms, and throws him down upon it with some violence. He now selects an assistant, who stations himself at the Dancer's left and begins to whet his knife on a stone. The other then grasps the muscles of the Dancer's breasts and pulls the flesh outward forcibly, while at his bidding the votary cries loudly and continuously, and holds a tuft of sage before his eyes, feigning tears; at the same moment the assistant, chewing a bit of sage, spits upon his knife, and thrusts it deliberately under the extended muscles. He next inserts the two skewers, pushing and twisting with considerable force. The Dancer is lifted to his feet, ever crying in a monotone utterly lacking in emotion; blood streams down his body; he is growing weak, and trembles as if about to fall. From the fork of the Mystery Tree dangle two plaited rawhide ropes, terminating in stout thongs, which are now slipped over the ends of the skewers. With his arms about the Dancer's body the assistant pulls him back four times, exerting his strength in drawing the loops tight. The Priest, chewing upon a bit of blue-flag root, now stands in front of the votary and spits toward his body and his face, imparting strength to him. Then after three long notes on his whistle, blown, as previously, beside and above the Dancer's head, he resumes his position at the latter's left, while the people shout their approval of the Sun Dancer's self-sacrifice.

Singers and dancers resume their functions; the Chief Dancer blows his bone whistle and extends his palm to the sun, throwing his weight upon the ropes in vain effort to tear himself loose, sometimes even leaping clear of the ground and letting himself fall back bodily. One song finished, the dancers turn to the south, and a little later to the west, following the course of the sun, right hands outstretched, whistles shrilling, voices wailing.

About mid-afternoon the Priest gives five small sticks to the Chief Dancer, who throws them among the spectators; each of the sticks is a token of a horse to be given by the Priest to the fortunate one who secures it. Then with his arms about the Dancer, he throws himself back in the endeavor to tear the skewers free; but by this time the flesh has so dried and hardened as to resist the strain, and the elastic rawhide ropes hurl them from their feet. If after four trials the flesh fails to give way, the Priest resumes his former station and fills a pipe, which he lays on the ground as a number of the Dancer's relations advance, each leading a horse packed with buffalo-robes, tanned skins, bags, or parfleches stuffed with pemmican. "We want you to cut the flesh of our boy," is their greeting. Then, while members of his own family take charge of the horses, the Priest bears the pipe to the man that assisted in piercing the Dancer, who accepts it and smokes, while the Priest throws off the ropes and lays the Dancer on his back. The assistant then cuts away the flesh, leaving a small part that can readily be torn through; and the Priest again raises the man to his feet and readjusts the ropes.

Once more the wild song bursts forth, and the Dancer, moving slowly at first as he summons all the energy of his weakened body, suddenly hurls himself back and falls helpless and unconscious as the skewers rend the flesh. The Priest lays him full on his back, while the assistant cuts away the ragged edges of the wounds. Again the song is taken up, the Dancer, again conscious, supporting himself upon a staff and swaying his body in rhythm.

It is now the time when other dancers may be pierced. Any one of them, wishing to make this offering to the sun, takes his pipe to one of the old men, who, after smoking, throws him down, pierces his breasts without ceremony, inserts the skewers, and adjusts the ropes. Such dancers are customarily not pierced deeply, but if one seeks the aid of a man who performed the more severe sacrifice of his body, he, too, must endure the same treatment as was meted out to the Chief Dancer. The self-torture continues until the sun sinks, some freeing themselves as the afternoon wears on, others requiring the added strength and weight of the Priest. Each, as he effects his release, rises and dances with what vigor he can summon. Frequently, as an additional sacrifice, a Sun Dancer has a number of buffalo-skulls, or even of buffalo-heads, attached by a rope to the muscles of his back; and there have been instances of suspending a man in mid-air by the muscles of the hips and shoulders.

As the sun nears the horizon a profusion of food is distributed among the spectators; but the dancers remain standing, gazing at the sun, and at the conclusion of the feast they return to their preparation tipis, the Priest accompanying the party of the Chief Dancer. After the sweat-bath, they sit side by side in the rear of the tipi, and the Priest, offering a piece of dog-meat to the Four Winds, the Sky, and the Earth, repeats a prayer:

"Great Mystery, you existed in the beginning. We have finished our ceremony. After you have eaten, these young men will partake of food. Give us help, that they may become strong and many."

The meat is put into the Chief Dancer's mouth, and other pieces are given to his companions; and after similar consecration, water is served to each one. The chiefs congregate in the tipi, and the feast of dog-meat and pemmican concludes the day.

"FOR STRENGTH AND VISIONS"

THE APSAROKE
Introduction

In assembling in the present volume the material pertaining to the Apsaroke and the Hidatsa, the original plan of treatment is not strictly followed; but since these two Siouan tribes were once united, the geographical grouping is sacrificed in this case to one based on close relationship. The separation of these people into two tribes occurred in such recent time that the knowledge of it is much more definite than tribal events usually are when their occurrence is known only by tradition; and, indeed, the dialectic differences between the two tribes are so unimportant as to establish the recency of the change. At no time has either tribe lost sight of its relationship to the other, and there has always existed a strong friendship between them.

A powerful tribe of mountaineers, subsisting entirely by the chase and quite independent of the uncertainties of agriculture, the Apsaroke regarded with more or less disdain their sedentary Hidatsa cousins, who tilled the soil and lacked the strength to carry on extensive predatory warfare. If the doughty No Vitals and his followers were agriculturists when they departed from the Missouri to seek a new home to the westward, they soon forgot their cunning in this industry and acquired contempt for an occupation so menial as tillage, for while nearly all the wandering tribes frowned on agriculture, the Apsaroke seemed to have been particularly averse to it.

In the Apsaroke is seen the highest development of the primitive American hunter and warrior. Physically these people were among the finest specimens of their race. They clothed themselves better and dwelt in larger and finer lodges than did their neighbors, and decked their horses in trappings so gorgeous as to arouse the wonder of all early explorers.

In gathering the material for this volume the writer has been fortunate in having the assistance of an interpreter possessing far more than ordinary ability; and fortunate indeed in enlisting the services of Hunts To Die, a veteran of unusual mentality, from whom was obtained a large part of the information respecting the Apsaroke herein recorded. Other old men of the tribe recounted myth, legend, and story of tribal life which served to confirm the knowledge communicated by Hunts To Die, but the effort of these to unfold the tribal lore may be likened to the attempt of an unthinking man to employ the utterances of a statesman. In early manhood Hunts To Die was a magnificent warrior, who scarcely knew his physical limitations; but at thirty years of age he was so seriously wounded by a Sioux bullet as to be barred from further action on the field of battle, yet he lives to make this portion of the story of the Indian more closely portray the primitive life than has been possible in the preceding volumes of the series.

The narrative of the vigorous life of the Apsaroke, of the camp, the hunt, the war-trail, and the cruel ordeals they underwent to invoke spiritual aid, contributes so much toward laying bare the inner life of this people that it is dwelt upon to the exclusion of folk-tales. Believing that by recording what and how the Indians think and see we can best add to our knowledge of them as a race, it has been the aim in presenting this material to reflect the thought and to preserve as nearly as possible the manner of expression of the narrators. Not alone therefore should the body of this volume give us a rare glimpse of the inner side of Apsaroke life, but the biographical sketches of the men whose portraits are presented, and whose lives are so strongly reflected in the modern history of the tribe, will add largely to our understanding of it.

Edward S. Curtis

THE OATH – APSAROKE

Fog In The Morning – Apsaroke

The Eagle Medicine-man – Apsaroke

Mother and Child – Apsaroke

BULL TONGUE – APSAROKE

MEDICINE LODGE - APSAROKE

APSAROKE WAR-CHIEF

SKINS WOLF — APSAROKE

The Eagle-Catcher

Big Ox – Apsaroke

OLD DOG – APSAROKE

TWO WHISTLES - APSAROKE

General Characteristics

In stature and in vigor the Apsaroke, or Crows, excelled all other tribes of the Rocky Mountain region, and were surpassed by none in bravery and in devotion to the supernatural forces that gave them strength against their enemies. Social laws, rigidly adhered to, prevented marriage of those even distantly related, and the hardships of their life as hunters eliminated infant weaklings. The rigors of this life made the women as strong as the men; and women who could carry a quarter of a buffalo apparently without great exertion, ride all day and all night with a raiding war-party, or travel afoot two hundred and fifty miles across an unmarked wilderness of mountains, plains, and swollen streams in four days and nights, were not the women to bring forth puny offspring.

The Apsaroke were and are the proudest of Indians, and although comparatively few (they now number only one thousand seven hundred and eighty-seven, and are constantly decreasing), they rarely allied themselves with other tribes for purposes of defence. For probably two and a half centuries they were the enemy of every tribe that came within striking distance, and for a goodly part of this time they were virtually surrounded by hostile bands with a common hatred against this mountain tribe that likened itself to a pack of wolves. The swarming thousands of the western Sioux, aided by the Cheyenne and Arapaho, tried to force them westward. The powerful Blackfeet invaded their territory from the north and northwest, Flatheads and Nez Perces were worthy foes from the west, and the wily Shoshoni pressed in from the south; yet the Apsaroke were ever ready to repel invasion from whatever direction it might come.

While the general status was one of hostility, there were brief intervals of peace with the different tribes, even with the Sioux, their bitterest foe, with whom at times they smoked the pipe and negotiated peace for a year. Such truces so seriously made in many smokes, were often quickly broken by some impetuous or irresponsible young man stealing a horse or a woman; then in a moment peace was at an end and conflict raged again. As a rule, however, these periods of tranquillity lasted long enough to permit discussion of previous fights and a general comparison of the honors therein won.

The country which the Apsaroke ranged and claimed as their own was an extensive one for so small a tribe. In area it may be compared, east and west, to the distance from Boston to Buffalo, and north to south, from Montreal to Washington — certainly a vast region to be dominated by a tribe never numbering more than fifteen hundred warriors. The borders of their range were, roughly, a line extending from the mouth of the Yellowstone southward through the Black Hills, thence westward to the crest of the Wind River mountains, northwestward through the Yellowstone Park to the site of Helena, thence to the junction of the Musselshell and the Missouri, and down the latter stream to the mouth of the Yellowstone. This region is the veritable Eden of the Northwest. With beautiful broad valleys and abundant wooded streams, no part of the country was more favorable for buffalo, while its wild forested mountains made it almost unequalled for elk and other highland game.

The Apsaroke enjoyed the climax of their existence during the scant century following the acquisition of horses. Previous to that event their life had not known the fulness that was theirs when they had herds of horses, and firearms had supplanted arrows and spears. Notwithstanding their aggressive, warlike disposition, they never were in serious conflict with the Government, nor did they commit many depredations against white settlers, who, although regarded by them as trespassers, were rarely molested. The Indians captured many horses from early hunters and trappers, but this was to them a legitimate procedure, for these men were intruders on their lands, taking their game, consequently all captures of livestock were regarded as just compensation.

By all observers who have written of them, the Crows have been pronounced exceedingly lax in morals, and while many statements of this sort have been overdrawn, they are certainly an unusually sensual people. Still, as an alien race, we should hardly presume to judge them wholly by our standards and not give them credit for their own customs and codes. They on their part consider some of our customs highly objectionable and immoral.

In the old times the Apsaroke, during a large part of the year, were constantly on the move. One day they would be quietly encamped on one of their favorite streams, the next travelling away in quest of buffalo or solely for the mere pleasure of going. Their customary camps were along the mountain streams, where the lodges were commonly placed in a circle, but at times, where the valley was narrow, they were close together, paralleling the wooded watercourse.

The larger camps were always the scene of great activity. Horses were tethered everywhere close at hand; on the slopes far and near thousands were grazing, while on the nearby hilltops groups of people were statuesquely outlined against the sky. Here are chiefs and councillors in quiet discussion of tribal affairs. As they pass the pipe from man to man and look down upon the village with its hundreds of lodges their eyes are glad, for the picture is one of plenty, and the murmur of the camp as it is wafted to their ears tells of happiness. Close by are laughing romping children, the bronze skin of their rounded bodies gleaming in the sunlight, and the old men reflect, "It is well that their bodies know the heat and the cold; it will make them strong warriors and mothers." On another hill proud youths are seen, decked in the savage trappings that make glad their hearts. Their words are of the hunt, the war-path, and sweethearts. Not far distant is a group of maidens gayly dressed in garments of soft skins. It is not many moons since they romped about with the freedom of fawns, unabashed that the breeze caressed their bodies; but all that is past now; they are maidens, every part save face and hands must be carefully concealed, and a keen-eyed mother is always near. But all cannot be childhood and youth and love-making; on other outlooks are wrinkled old women who live only in the past, muttering and dreaming of the days of their youth, when husbands and sweethearts rode away to conflict, — of the days when brave warriors stole them from the arms of others, — when warrior husbands took them along on their forays, perhaps to see their men killed and themselves borne off by the victorious Lakota, on whose coup-sticks waved the hair upon which they had lavished so much loving attention. Further from the village mourners cry out in anguish for those whose lives have been taken; and on distant peaks are lonely men fasting through the long days and nights in supplication for spiritual strength.

In the camp itself there is an endless panorama of activities and a ceaseless confusion of sounds. Women are everywhere stretching the drying hides, and filling great drying-racks with long thin strips of rich, red buffalo-meat. In the lodges others are tanning skins, and on many sides can be heard the thud of the wooden tray as women gamble with plum-seed dice. In other lodges men are shouting a wild song as they engage in the hand gambling game, while in the open another group is playing at hoop-and-pole, and others the game of the arrows. The sick and the wounded are being cared for by medicine-men, who accompany their incantation with rattle and drum. Men and women, old and young, are constantly passing from lodge to lodge for a word or a smoke, and food is always placed before them.

As evening approaches the people begin to gather around the lodge-fires, and with the arrival of men laden with the product of the hunt, the village assumes an even livelier air. Heralds of the chiefs are shouting invitations to the feasts, and as night falls the lodges glow in the darkness. If the weather is at all cool, the evening is spent mostly indoors, where on soft skins and furs heaped in profusion, the people lounge in full contentment. From many dwellings echo the muffled beat of the drum and the droning song of men and women, and occasionally is heard the doleful note of a flute as some love-sick youth serenades his sweetheart.

Early in the morning the village is astir, for the counsel of the men who have thoughts is, "Do not follow the sleep to the end, but waken when it requires determination; be up and alive to what is going on about you!" As soon as the family awaken they throw blankets around their bodies and go to the river for their morning bath. If the water is icy cold, so much the better, for it requires a strong heart to plunge in, and it inures the body to cold and heat. Husband and wife and small children go together, each family a group of itself. Probably not ten yards away is another family, and so on for a smile or more, many hundreds bathing at the same time. At other hours of the day it would be the height of impropriety for a woman to expose any part of her body, but at the morning bath there is no embarrassment, "for this is our custom," they say. Truly custom is a strange thing, for an Apsaroke woman — who a half-hour before has been playing about in the water like a happy seal — blushes at the picture of a white woman in a decollete gown, and says, "Such women have no shame!" Parties of maidens, accompanied by some watchful mother, bathe in secluded nooks.

When the chief decides that camp is to be moved, his herald goes through the village in the evening, crying out, "Prepare, prepare! To-morrow we move!" And again at the first blush of day he rides from end to end of the village, calling, *Hunhunheeeeeee! To-day the chief says we move toward the buffalo! Men, bring in the horses; women, throw down the lodges!"* As all have known from the previous announcement that they are to move, the morning meal is finished before daylight appears. Soon all the herds of horses come trotting in and the women are running about among them throwing ropes over the necks of the old, gentle pack-animals. Others are at work on the lodges, the covers of which come rattling down, soon making of the camp a skeleton of bare poles. From the middle of each framework a column of smoke curls skyward; sleepy children still in their blankets are rolled out as their mothers pull the robes from under them in the work of packing. The tousled-headed youngsters whimper for something to eat and are thrown a hard, dry piece of meat for their breakfast. Soon the horses are packed with high bundles of robes and clothing, and the lodge-poles tied at the sides, usually six to a side, two horses being required for each lodge. Here and there horses break away and go galloping through the camp before their packs are secured, scattering their loads broadcast, and causing great excitement and

99

confusion. Women call, children cry, grandmothers chatter and mumble.

The chief rides off a short distance in the direction they are to go, and some of his old men sit about him smoking and talking. Then they move forward a distance and halt while the people complete their preparations for the march. Now the line begins to form – first the chiefs and old men; then a band of arrogant, gayly dressed Lumpwoods, with newly stolen wives riding behind and carrying their husbands' shields and lances; next a body of clansmen with a group of proud young wives bedecked in all their finery. Behind them the column continues to form, family by family, each driving its herd of horses, until at length come straggling by those who have been slow in packing. A moving column of six hundred lodges is miles in length and of a width determined by the groups of families or by the nature of the country traversed. When they near the place the chief has designated for the night's camp, many of the grandfathers ride ahead and select spots for their own lodges, clear the ground, and gather dry wood. As the irregular line drags in, they stand beside their chosen places, calling out to their wives where to come. If the weather be cold, they already have kindled small fires, and now take down the little children from the tops of the packs and hold them in the warmth of the leaping flames.

A splendid picture of the nomads' life they made as the caravan moved across far-reaching plain, hill, and valley. The crossing of a broad stream added much to the animation of the scene. One summer nine hundred and fifty lodges of Apsaroke went to the Yellowstone, intending to cross. As the water was very high and the river nearly half a mile in width, the Kick Bellys, numbering four hundred and fifty lodges, lost their courage, and would not attempt the crossing. All the others, however, were unafraid and passed over. They used no boats, but made small rafts of driftwood, laying the ends of the lodge-poles on these rude craft, and allowing the tops to float on the water behind. On the poles a large piece of old lodge-covering was spread, and on that were piled the domestic belongings, the edges of the skin being gathered up and tied at the top to protect the load from splashing water. Perched upon

100

this bundle rode the old women and the children. Two young men grasped the manes of strong swimming horses and swam along by their side, towing the raft across. Behind, holding to the ends of the lodge-poles, swam the young women and maidens, clad only in a short skirt reaching from waist to knee. It was a time of great merriment and fun-making, yet one not without its serious side, for a tottering old woman gazed long at the swirling river and, declaring that she was not afraid to die but feared the water, stabbed herself and fell lifeless. The crossing occupied four days, for the current was swift, and many who had no horses were compelled to wait for assistance from their relatives. Before going into the water men and women painted red stripes about waist, wrists, and ankles, for protection against the water-monsters that were believed to inhabit all large streams. Necklaces of white beads were never worn in the water, for beads of that sort were believed to be hailstones, the symbol of the Thunderbird, a deadly enemy of water-monsters, which therefore would be glad to swallow any one thus showing his friendship with the Thunderbird.

SPIRIT BEINGS

Itsihbadhish, He First Made All Things, is the creator of all. He is composed of all the vapory elements that existed before the world was formed by him. He is also called *Akbahiutsedhete,* He That Sees All Things. He made all things, he hears all things, he controls all things, and is everywhere present. The sun itself is usually conceived to be his visible counterpart, and even in the legends that personify the sun as a distinct spirit-power it is regarded as under the control of its creator. The old people sometimes say, "See this light that comes into the lodge: He That Hears Always is in it." The perceptions of Itsihbadhish do not end with men, animals and noticeable phenomena, but extend to the insects and the most insignificant things of plant life. In him, the personification and deification of the infinite, the Apsaroke have crystallized their religious instinct; and while every creature has its spiritual comple-

101

ment, and many objects and elements are specifically personified, these all are under the control of Itsihbadhish.

Every star, the sun, the moon, the sky itself, every tree, stone, stream, animal, insect, and bird, every natural phenomenon, has its spirit above. These spirits may or may not exert supernatural power, but such as do are called *mahpe,* while all considered collectively are *mawahpe.* This term does not, however, include He First Made All Things, who is *Mawahpakashe,* "the real *mawahpe.*" The *mawahpe* are often called *Mahodhete,* Those That Have No Bodies, and their earthly representatives are described as *Maishpidhadhete,* Those That Have No Fires.

The spirit that talks to the soul in vision and gives it strength becomes one's *hupadhiu* (with first personal pronoun, *biyuhpadhiu*), medicine, or tutelary spirit. Through visions men and women claim to have revealed to them events of the future, and how they shall conduct themselves to better their own lives and to promote the welcome of their people. Visions are experienced by those who fast in the mountains, and are not in any way to be confused with dreams. When a man fasts, he wails, "He That Hears Always, hear my cries. As my tears drop to the ground, look upon me." While he moans thus in his despair, he grovels on the earth and tears up grass and weeds in anguish of spirit. Then he hacks off a finger tip, or very frequently he cuts around the second joint, puts the finger between his teeth, and tears it off; then holding the severed portion to the sky, he cries, "*Mawahpe* [supernatural powers], I give you this, my body. May I have many horses, and many women of good looks and industry in my lodge. May my lodge be the gathering place of men. I am poor; give me these things that through me my people may be bold because I live. Let them use me as a shield against the enemy!"

While the body of the faster sleeps, there comes to the soul *Akbatsivekyati,* Little One That Tells Things, a spirit so small as to be invisible even to the soul. It stands behind the ear and instructs the soul what it shall look for; as for example, "When he comes, watch his feet. See how many steps he takes

102

for each act." While no one has ever seen one of these spirits, of which each *mahpe* has one as its messenger, all men that have had clear visions have heard their voices. Following Akbatsivekyati appears the earthly representative of the spirit that has chosen the faster for his child, and either tells the soul all that the spirit wishes to say, or merely announces that the father himself is coming to bestow his powers. After the spirit or its representative has minutely described the way the faster is to conduct himself, — to paint, to dress, to sing, what plants to gather if he is a medicine-man, what things he is to avoid, — the soul returns to the body and informs it of these things; or, as some express it, "Perhaps the conversation takes place in the heart of the faster, and he knows what is being said."

Sometimes, but by no means always, the spirit that becomes one's *hupadhiu*, if it finds its child worthy, enters the body and lives with the soul, and is then called *batsidhupe*.

A man may have more than one *hupadhiu*, obtained either by fastings or by purchase. If medicine is bought, he then must go out and fast, and the appearance of its spirit in a vision assures him that he has been accepted. If it does not appear, then it does not desire him and will not aid him; still he keeps the medicine, and tries again to obtain its power. The symbol of one's spirit is worn usually in the hair, and beside that the paint and the incense and other herbs revealed by it are constantly carried, wrapped in a piece of deerskin enclosed in rawhide. Since the great supernatural power hears all things, a man never falsely claims a vision, for such an act would incur the anger of Itsihbadhish, and he would probably lose his life, or some other great calamity would befall him.

If wilfully or inadvertently a man commits an act that might displease his tutelary spirit, he at once makes offerings and prays that it may not withdraw its aid. All success in life is attributed to one's spirit guardians, and to exhibit pride or take personal credit for one's welfare would be to offend *mawahpe* and result in misfortune.

GOES AHEAD — APSAROKE

"CRYING TO THE SPIRITS"